Heart Maps

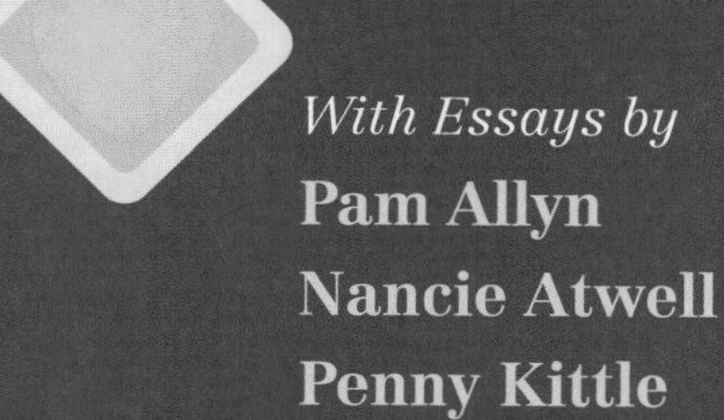

Georgia Heard

With Essays by
Pam Allyn
Nancie Atwell
Penny Kittle

HeartMaps

Helping Students Create and Craft Authentic Writing

20 Heart Map Templates to Inspire and Engage Writers

HEINEMANN
Portsmouth, NH

Heinemann
361 Hanover Street
Portsmouth, NH 03801–3912
www.heinemann.com

Offices and agents throughout the world

The author and publisher wish to thank those who have generously given permission to reprint borrowed material:

"When Someone Deeply Listens to You" by John Fox was reprinted with permission from the author.

Figures 5.29 and 5.30: From *In the Middle*, Third Edition, by Nancie Atwell. Copyright © 2015 by Nancie Atwell. Published by Heinemann, Portsmouth, NH. All rights reserved.

Cataloging-in-Publication Data is on file at the Library of Congress.
ISBN: 978-0-325-07449-8

Editor: Zoë Ryder White
Production: Hilary Goff
Cover and interior designs: Suzanne Heiser
Typesetter: Eric Rosenbloom, Kirby Mountain Composition
Manufacturing: Steve Bernier

Printed in the United States of America on acid-free paper

20 19 18 17 16 VP 1 2 3 4 5

For my mother, who taught me that a home with books is a home with heart.

Contents

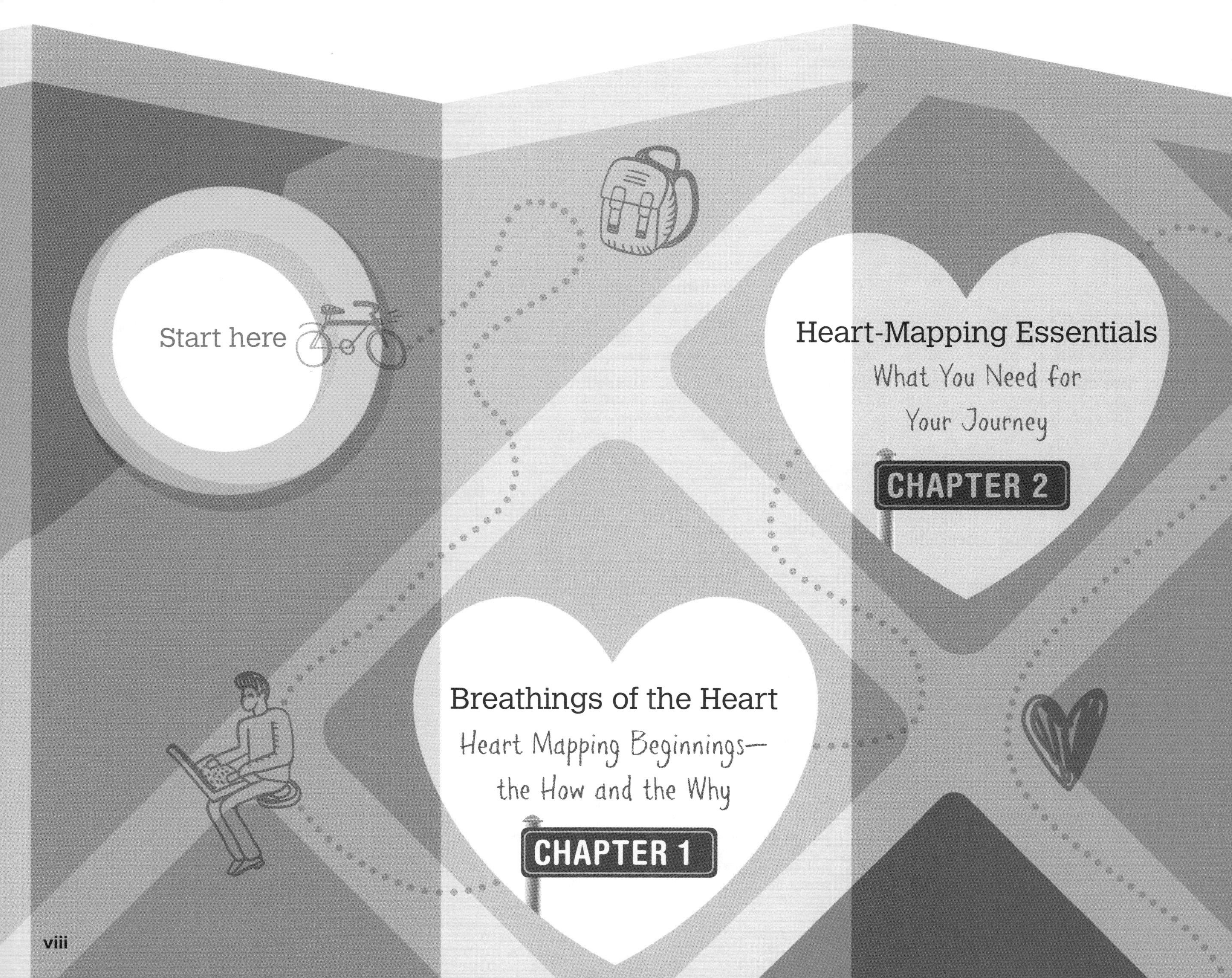
Start here
Heart-Mapping Essentials
What You Need for Your Journey
CHAPTER 2
Breathings of the Heart
Heart Mapping Beginnings—the How and the Why
CHAPTER 1

CHAPTER 3

The Heart of the Matter

20 Heart Maps to Inspire and Engage Writers

Breathtakingly beautiful children's heart maps filled with hope and caring

CHAPTER 5

Three Hearts

Guest Essays

CHAPTER 4

Digging Deeper

Sharing, Reflecting on, and Writing from Heart Maps

Acknowledgments

Dermot
for awakening my heart.
Leo *for deepening my heart.*
Zoë Ryder White *editor extraordinaire!*
Katie Wood Ray *for a new vision of my book.*
Pam Allyn, *founder and director of LitWorld and LitClubs, for "LitWorld Heart Stories" and for your passion in transforming children's lives through literacy.* **Ana Seastone Stern**, *international program director of LitWorld, for shepherding the amazing Spring Heart Mapping Initiative. The* **directors of LitClubs around the world and the partner organizations and all the beautiful openhearted children who shared their maps.** ♧ **Nancie Atwell**, *and the* **Center for Teaching and Learning**, *for always reminding us what matters.* **Penny Kittle** *for "Tune in to Your Heart Map Playlist" and for tirelessly helping teens believe that words have the power to make things happen.* **Mary Glover**, *founder and teacher at the Awakening Seed School, who celebrates the poetry in every child and creature on this earth. For* **students at the Awakening Seed School** *who mapped their hearts so deeply and honestly.* **Bev Gallagher**, *and her wonderful students, for your warmth and enthusiasm and for always imagining the possibilities.* **Margaret Simon** *and the* **children from Iberia Parish Gifted Program** *for your beautiful maps and blog writing. For the* **teachers and students at PS 29**, *thank you for mapping your hearts with such enthusiasm and passion:* **Kristin Beers**, **Jessica Albizu**, **Lynn Manna**. *For the* **children and teachers at Princeton Junior School** *for your zest in exploring heart maps and for the lively Skype conversations:* **Silvana Clark**, **Anne Korsen**, **Colleen Nelson**, **Susan Weintraub**. ♧ **Kristin Ackerman** *and her class of* **third graders at The Benjamin School** *for diving deep into the world of heart mapping and nonfiction.* **Kim Haines** *and the* **children of Alexander Dawson School** *for your colorful and delightful heart maps.* **Mrs. Tallman** *and the* **children of Oliver Wendell Holmes Elementary** *for your decorative and lovely heart maps.* **Melanie Cravey** *and her* **students at Bee Cave Elementary School** *for your creative and earnest heart maps.* **Diane Sullivan** *and her students for your artistic heart maps.* ♧ **Amy Clark** *for all the extraordinary books and resources.*
For the miraculous Heinemann team:
Amanda Bondi, *editorial coordinator;*
Hilary Goff, *production editor;*
Suzanne Heiser, *designer;*
Elizabeth Tripp, *copyeditor;*
Lisa Fowler, *VP and Publisher.*

1

Breathings of the Heart

Heart Mapping Beginnings—the How and the Why

Hanging on the wall in my childhood house was an antique world map. Off in the right-hand corner, a schooner, masts in full sail, crossed an ocean. I often wondered where the ship was going and what the world was like when it got there. Maps gave me a sense of what was possible. Beyond my house, my neighborhood, and my town (Alexandria, Virginia), I saw a bigger world: oceans and countries that I had never heard of. Looking at that map as I passed by, I dreamed of sailing away to a life of exploration and adventure.

When I grew up, my older sister and two cousins became mapmakers and worked at the National Geographic Society. My grandmother promised to pay my way through college if I got a degree in cartography. It was tempting. I declined her offer, however; I became a writer, poet, and teacher of writing instead. Now I think of myself as a cartographer of the heart: mapping out inner territories with words—and helping others do the same.

Daniele Quercia (2014), a computer scientist and inventor of what he calls "happy maps," says, "Maps are associated with efficiency. We take out our mobile app and it will show us the shortest, most efficient route from point A to point B. But what about a map that routes us the most beautiful way, or the quietest way, or a route that has the most personal memories?" He calls happy maps "a cartography weighted for human emotions." Similarly, writing is sometimes taught as an efficient stringing together of words and sentences or an exercise in grammatical skills. *Heart mapping* is a metaphor for what all writers know: to write is to delve into what matters to us, to keep our feelings alive, to be vulnerable, to tell the truth, to question, and to speak what many people only keep inside. Writing is also *weighted for human emotions.*

I was puzzling over the idea of mapping the heart long before I first introduced it to the classroom. I wrote about imagining a metaphoric heart map as a means to discover stories.

Fill your paper with the breathings of your heart.

—William Wordsworth

> Finding home is crucial to the act of writing. Begin here. With what you know. With the tales you've told dozens of times to friends or a spouse or a lover. *With the map you've already made in your heart*. (1995, 2; italics added)

Heart Mapping with Children

Years later, as a visiting writer in a school in Phoenix, Arizona, I began a heart-mapping project with third-grade writers. My goal was to inspire them to write honest, thoughtful poems—to show them that writing can give voice to our most secret, true selves. In the following excerpt from my book *Awakening the Heart: Exploring Poetry in Elementary and Middle School*, I introduce the idea of using heart mapping to kindle writing ideas for the first time.

> I gathered the third graders on the rug and told them how poets write from their hearts about what we deeply care about. I told them that I write my poems from memories of my family, of growing up next to a creek in Virginia, and of the people I meet in my travels. Hands started to go up one by one, as kids were eager to tell their own important memory or something close to their hearts. After a few poets had shared I felt they understood where poems come from, so I sent them back to their tables to write their poems. As they hunched over their papers, writing, I walked around the room to read their poems. I glanced over Lacrisha's shoulder. Her poem went like this:
>
> *Money, money, money is nice.*
> *Money, money, money is good.*
> *I like money.*
>
> I moved along and glanced at other poems, "I like to play Nintendo after school. It's really, really fun." Most of the poems were quick sentences about what they liked but I didn't sense much heartfelt poetry. I knew I had to do something drastic.
>
> The next day when I gathered the class together again I said, "Remember yesterday how we talked about that poets write from their hearts—what we really care about?" A few heads nodded, "Well, I was thinking last night that sometimes poets have to do some work first to know what's really in their hearts, to know what they really care about, and what's really important to them. So today, we're going to do something very different—we're going to make maps of our hearts."
>
> I heard a few whispers, "Maps of our hearts! What's that?"
>
> "Today, I'd like you to make a map of all the important things that are in your heart, all the things that really matter to you. You can put: people and places that you care about; moments and memories that have stayed with you; things you love to do; anything that has stayed in your heart because you care about it. First, let's sit for

a while, and I'd like you to think about what might go in the map of your heart."

. . .

They shared a few ideas: grandmothers and grandfathers who had died; learning to sing; love felt for dogs, cats, and other pets; divorced parents; newly born brothers and sisters. They returned to their tables with colored pencils and white art paper to begin mapping their hearts.

Once they began to draw and write, their hearts were amazing.
(1999, 108)

Since then, I've introduced heart mapping to hundreds of writers of all ages as a way not only to dig deep into ideas for writing poems but also to spark different genres—personal narrative, nonfiction, essay—and to guide revision. Young writers from all over the world have mapped their hearts with courage and honesty, and through the process they have found their way into writing that deeply matters to them.

I've kept the stories and faces of my students with me since that first day. What follows are several students' heart maps and stories that have touched me deeply over the years.

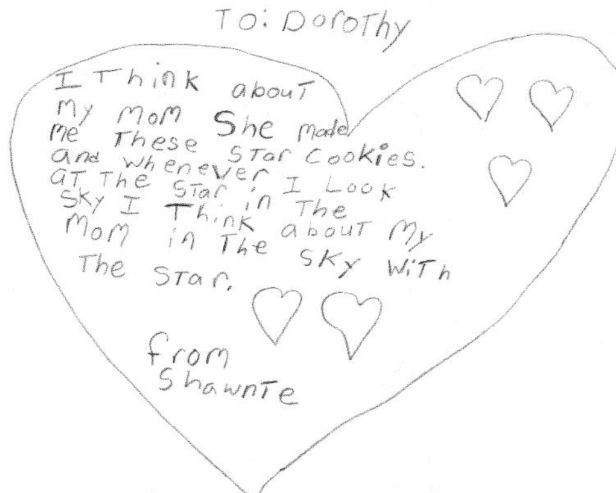

Figure 1.1 I love how Shawnte dedicates her heart map to her mother, Dorothy. She uses beautiful imagery with the repetition of *star cookies* and *stars in the sky*.

Opening Hearts: Three Heart-Mapping Stories

Shawnte was a student at a special education school in Queens, New York. She had a thin, fragile-looking face and dark circles under her eyes. She looked worried and I rarely saw her smile. "She never writes," her teacher told me. After introducing heart mapping to Shawnte's class, I watched as students began to draw pictures inside their heart maps. Shawnte drew a heart on her paper and immediately started to write inside it a short poem about her mother, Dorothy, who had passed away a few years before (see Figure 1.1).

Shawnte didn't stop there. She wrote dozens of stories and poems about her mother, and the glimpse of childhood she remembered, all within the heart map format. It was a concrete, visual, and safe way to explore her powerful and sad feelings. (See Figure 1.2.)

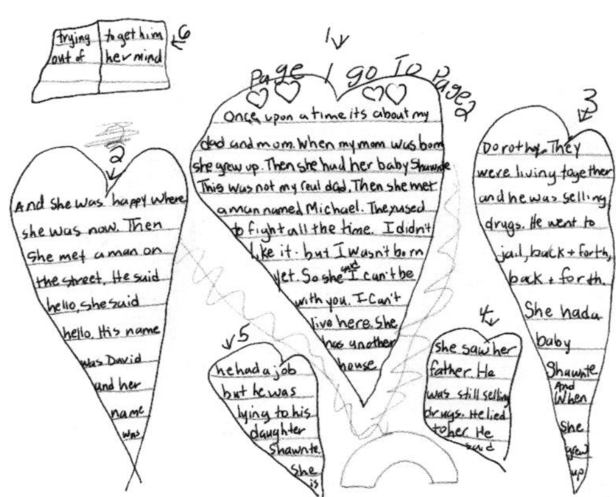

Figure 1.2 Shawnte's story written on multiple heart maps

My latin heart My American heart
My heart is falling
cómo un petalo le rosa enlatierra
My heart its going crazy
como un loco sin rumbo
My heart its scared
como un niño sin sus padres
My heart its lonely
Como una telaraña en micuarto
My heart its in love
con la niña que nunca vendra
But I guess if I try my best
my corazón se curara.

Figure 1.3 Gaspar writes his poem in alternating lines of English and Spanish, *telling* how he feels in English and then on the next line *showing* us how he feels in Spanish.

Gaspar was a bilingual eighth-grade student near Phoenix, Arizona, with jet-black hair, a round face, and a quick smile. When he drew his heart map he divided it in the middle, which, he told me later, symbolized his two worlds—his bilingual world: Mexico, where he was born, and his new American world. Gaspar sat at his desk, looking at his divided heart, and then suddenly grabbed a piece of paper and wrote a poem, half in English and half in Spanish, to express the split he felt between his two worlds. Through imagery and figurative language, he was able to show the emotional divide he felt between his two worlds (see Figure 1.3).

My Latin Heart My American Heart

My heart is falling
como un petalo le rosa en la tierra
(*like a rose petal on the ground*)
My heart its going crazy
como un loco sin rumbo
(*like feeling crazy without direction*)
My heart its scared
como un niño sin sus padres
(*like a child without parents*)
My heart its lonely
como una telaraña en micuarto
(*like a spider web in my room*)
My heart its in love
con la niña que nunca vendra
(*like the girl that will never come*)
But I guess if I try my best
my corazón se curare (*my heart will heal*).

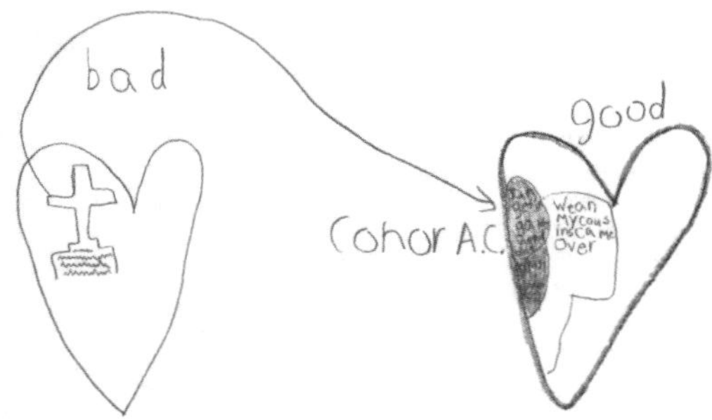

Figure 1.4 Conor's bad and good hearts

Conor, a second grader in New York, sat on the rug quietly, hands folded in his lap, almost invisible as I explained heart mapping to the class. When he returned to his desk, he drew two hearts on his paper. When I conferred with him, he told me, "This is when my dad died. I drew an arrow to *good* because I'm getting a new good dad, and I like it when my cousins come over. I drew the bad one in black. I didn't like those times. The good heart is in red." (See Figure 1.4.)

Conor was the first writer to create more than one heart to represent his good and bad feelings.

How Heart Mapping Nurtures Writers

Recently I typed "heart mapping and writing" into Google and over five million entries popped up, including these:

- Writing from the Heart
- How to Start Writer's Workshop with Heart Maps
- Heart Mapping and Writing Territories
- Personal Narrative Heart Mapping

And my two favorites:

- Forget Following Your Heart: Follow Your Heartbreak
- Bespoke Map Heart Artwork (a site that sells heart maps)

If you type "heart mapping" into Pinterest, you can view hundreds of inspiring examples of heart maps from classrooms all over the world.

Since that first heart-mapping experience, my work with heart mapping and writing has expanded and deepened. Recently, with the adoption of the Common Core State Standards and states' own versions of the CCSS, the voices of those who want to shift writing in schools away from the personal toward the academic and impersonal have become louder. But writers know that all writing, no matter what genre, is in some sense personal and that by digging inside to excavate topics that matter, we inevitably express our opinions, voices, and feelings. Heart mapping is a way to acknowledge and nurture this truth about writing.

In addition to teaching the *how* of writing (the craft and the conventions), I think we need to pay equal attention to the *why*:

- What motivates us to write?
- What makes us care deeply about writing so much so that we spend hours and days revising to get our words just right?
- How can we help our students "ache with caring," as Mem Fox writes, about their writing?

The writer Lee Martin (2011) invites his writing students to first discover what matters to them. He writes, "We spend so many hours laboring over . . . craft. . . . Shouldn't we be devoting all that time to material that's significant to us?"

Six Reasons for Heart Mapping

1. **Authentic writing comes from the heart.** Heart mapping gives students a chance to explore what's in their hearts and to explore how they feel, what they're passionate about, and what they deeply care about. William Stafford wrote, "Once someone said to me, 'Think of something that happened, but don't tell what happened. . . . Try to remember more of your feelings than just the look of things; tell how they felt'" (1990, 59). Heart mapping helps writers write from the inside out and explore questions like "How did it feel to me?" and "What's the heart of my story?" Poets and fiction writers are not the only writers to tap into their feelings; contrary to what many people believe, nonfiction writers do so as well. The biographer David McCullough (1999) says, "*I* want to get inside the events and feel what it was like. People often ask me if I'm 'working on a book,' and I say yes . . . but in fact they've got the wrong preposition. I'm *in* the book, *in* the subject, *in* the time and the place." Milton Meltzer, a historian and nonfiction writer, reiterates McCullough's belief: "In the writer who cares, there is a pressure of feelings which emerges in the rhythm of sentences, in the choice of details, and in the color of the language" (1976).

   No matter what genre, our best writing comes from getting at the heart of the story or topic.

2. **Heart mapping opens the door to literacy for all writers — including reluctant, struggling, and blocked writers.** Heart mapping is a cure for writer's block. Many things can interfere with telling our stories. Sometimes we think we're too busy or we have too much on our minds, but often the real roadblock is our inner critic judging our words harshly, telling us to *keep quiet*. As teachers, we have a responsibility to carefully tend to our students' writing voices. I've been told many stories of the way some teachers' unthinking harshness deeply affected a new writer's confidence — one professor actually said to a teacher, "You should never even think about being a writer." Eventually, many would-be writers lose touch with their inner voices and their stories go untold. Heart mapping becomes an invitation to collect stories, memories, feelings, and ideas, without the whisperings of that critical voice.

   Maybe it's easier to write from heart maps because they are concrete and visual, or maybe because there are no conventional rules, or perhaps it's because writers tend to be more focused on writing what matters than on grammar or spelling. Although there is quite a bit of writing involved in heart mapping, not one student, no matter how reluctant a writer he or she was, has ever said to me, "I can't think of what to write in my heart map," or "I can't spell, so I can't make a heart map."

3. **Heart maps can function as a practical touchstone for writers.** As writers reread and reflect on the completed heart maps taped into their writers' notebooks or displayed on classroom walls, they find that a heart map can be a practical and useful tool for writing throughout the year. The maps spark new ideas, help overcome writer's block, and remind students what's important as they search for writing ideas.

4. **Heart mapping taps into the power of visual learning.** An article in *Psychology Today* states, "Our brain is mainly an image processor. Much of our sensory cortex is devoted to vision" (Kourndian 2012). Because writing is contained within the visual shape of a heart, it tends to be less abstract and becomes a kind of visual and emotional blueprint for writers to map the people, memories, and experiences that are significant and memorable to them.

5. **Heart mapping gives writers the freedom to explore and allows an idea or image room to grow.** David Bartholomae writes, "In assignment after assignment, we find students asked to reduce a novel, a poem, or their own experience into a single sentence, and then to use the act of writing in order to defend or 'support' that single sentence. *Writing is used to close a subject down rather than open it up*, to put an end to discourse rather than open up a project" (1983; italics added). The five-paragraph essay format, or any restrictive writing formula, can lock down writing, become limiting for writers, and make writing dull and lifeless. Referring back to the map metaphor, a GPS, like the five-paragraph essay format, may direct us by the most efficient route, but it also assumes that we know where we are going. Heart mapping is a scaffold that supports writers as they brainstorm, play (yes, play!), take wrong turns, search for the right words, and generate multiple ideas to open up a topic.

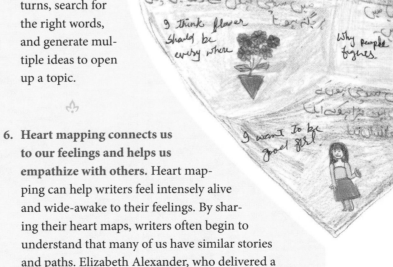

6. **Heart mapping connects us to our feelings and helps us empathize with others.** Heart mapping can help writers feel intensely alive and wide-awake to their feelings. By sharing their heart maps, writers often begin to understand that many of us have similar stories and paths. Elizabeth Alexander, who delivered a poem at Obama's inauguration in 2009, wrote a

book of poems when she was left to raise two sons alone after her husband's unexpected death. Michelle Obama spoke of Alexander's advice to all who have experienced the loss of someone we love: "It's Elizabeth's way of telling us all, 'You are not alone, you will eventually find your way to the other side, and the love you felt for the one you lost will ultimately be your salvation'" (Superville 2015). No matter what our life stories are, heart mapping and sharing our heart maps can help us recognize that all of us have life stories in common.

I've been touched by the variety and beauty of students' heart maps in my work with writing and heart mapping. Heart maps are visual representations of writers' hearts, but they are also vehicles to express something foundational about our identities. My hope is that this book can help our thinking about how to engage writers in finding purpose and passion in their writing and to help them *ache with caring*.

2

Heart-Mapping Essentials

What You Need for Your Journey

Find what causes a commotion in your heart. Find a way to write about that.

—Richard Ford

Bookstores are filled with travel guides on how to help plan your journey to a new country or city. Heart mapping is a journey for which you don't have to pack your suitcase, get in a car, or board a plane. For twenty years I've been a tour guide of sorts for hundreds of heart-mapping writers; all you need is paper, pen, an open heart, and a willingness to explore what matters to you. I do have a few practical tips on how to navigate this heart-mapping journey in the classroom.

How to Introduce Heart Mapping

Share your own heart map with your students. It will not only inspire them but also help you understand how to help those who find this invitation challenging.

In my heart map (see Figure 2.1), my husband, son, dog, and extended family are in the center of my heart. Surrounding the center are friends, places, art, writing, reading, and so on. I usually try not to think too much when creating a heart map; instead, I open my heart and let what's important find its way onto the page.

Use one of the twenty heart map templates in Chapter 3 to get started, or create your own. Place your heart map on a chart or underneath a document camera, and think aloud as you add to it. You can begin at the center of your heart, like I did, placing the most important persons, places, and things in the middle, and then work your way out toward the edges, talking to writers about your choices. Share stories and small details. Share surprises, discoveries, and feelings as you map your heart.

You might also use a mentor text like Sara Fanelli's *My Map Book* (2001), a beautifully illustrated picture book that walks the reader through a variety of vividly illustrated maps of the author's life—a neighborhood map, a map of her face, and a map of her heart. Fanelli includes large categories on her heart map, like *Friends*, *Sunny Days*, and *Nice*

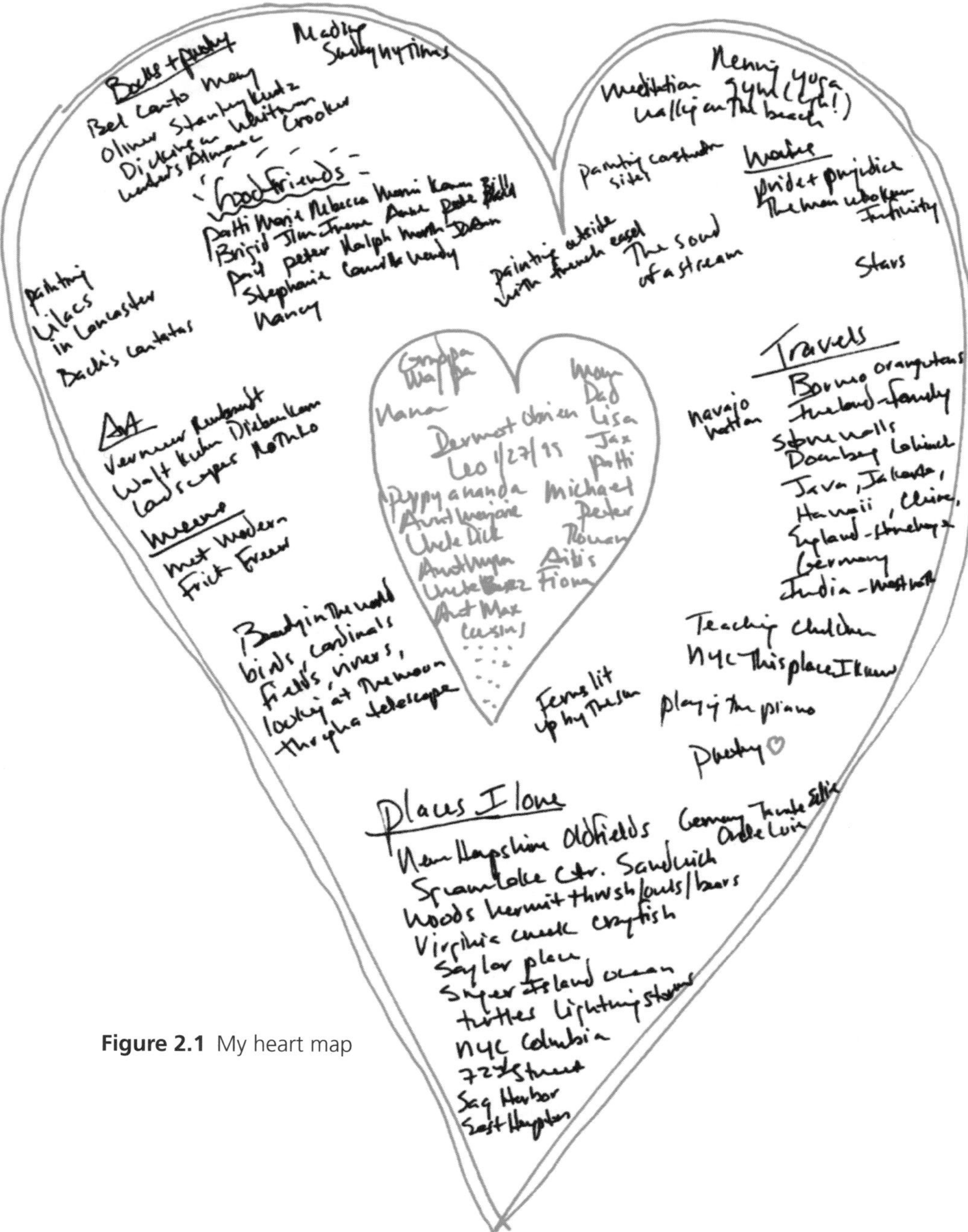

Figure 2.1 My heart map

Surprises, ready to be cracked open with detailed stories and images.

Share heart maps by other students, such as the beautiful maps in this book or the hundreds of student heart maps available on the Internet (google "heart mapping and writing" or search on Pinterest).

Before students work independently, ask them to brainstorm the content of their own heart maps and their design choices as well: Will they draw, write, or both? Where will they place each idea? (See Chapter 3 for more ideas on designing and writing heart maps.)

After modeling heart mapping with the whole group, you might invite writers to explore one of the twenty heart map templates in Chapter 3, whichever map fits best with your class' needs.

When to Introduce Heart Mapping

The earlier in the year you introduce heart mapping, the sooner writers will discover writing ideas that will inspire and engage them. If writers keep notebooks, they can keep heart maps there and refer to them for writing ideas throughout the year.

If you use a writing workshop model, and your writing curriculum consists of genre units of study, you can introduce heart mapping at the beginning of any genre study simply by adding an extra day or two at the beginning of the unit of study.

Some teachers have implemented heart-mapping Mondays (or any day during the week) throughout the year.

Writers can also work on their heart maps when they first come in in the morning, as they're waiting for class to begin, or at the end of the day.

What to Include on Heart Maps

Six Flags theme park? Strawberry ice cream? Chocolate? Writers often ask me if they should include a particular experience or thing on their heart maps. My answer is always, "It's your heart map. You're in charge of what you place on it. Only you know what's stored in your heart and whether or not to include it on your heart map."

How do writers decide what to include and what to leave out of their heart maps? If they're not sure if something belongs, suggest they write their entries in pencil first and then decide later if each addition belongs. Writers can always create a more permanent heart map later using markers and pens.

Thinking through where to place things on a heart map is also part of the journey. Some writers place less important things around the edges of their hearts, or even outside their hearts, and place the most significant things in the center. In her heart map, Lenette included nonessentials and dislikes outside the frame of her heart (*spiders*; *people that make you cry*; *mean people*; *cheese*; *snakes*; and *fighting with my sister*) and placed what she loved on the inside (see Figure 2.2).

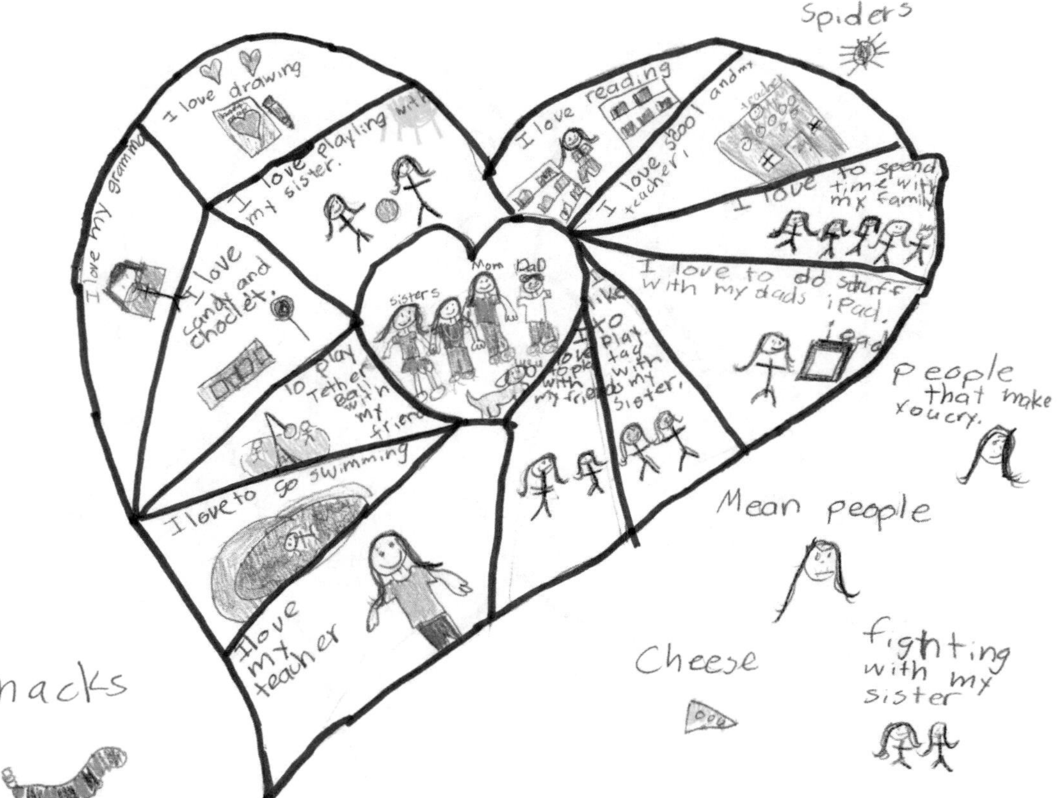

Figure 2.2 Lenette's heart map

Justin wrote and drew his dislikes and what was not as important outside his heart: *pink in my meat*; *vegetables*; *color pink*; *color yellow*; *snakes*; *peppers*; and *frogs*; *tacos*; *burritos*; *tamales*; and *root beer soda* (see Figure 2.3).

What stays inside and outside the heart will change depending on what heart map you're using from Chapter 3.

Figure 2.3 Justin's heart map

Time Needed for Heart Maps

Time. It's what we talk a lot about these days both in school and in our lives. How do we find time for what really matters? I believe *how* is linked to *why*. If we truly believe something is important, we will make time for it. Robert Grudin, author of *The Grace of Great Things: Creativity and Innovation*, writes about how creative people make use of time:

> Creative people move purposefully across this continent [of time], truly explore it. The rest of us shack up in little patches and clearings of time, always harried, always distracted, slave to the next knock on the office door or phone call. Our professional lives show an alarmingly high percentage of "response activities"—meeting deadlines, obeying directives. . . . Creative activity demands the opposite. (1990, 83)

How can we *not* make time for heart mapping when we know it will help *all* writers go deeper in their writing? (See more reasons for heart mapping in Chapter 1.)

You can invite writers to live with their heart maps over a few days and add to their heart maps little by little as they're inspired. Or devote an hour, a day, or a month to heart mapping. Writers can sketch entries on their heart maps on one day and reread and decide what to keep and delete on another. Another day, they can elaborate on their writing. Writers will also need time to reflect on, share, and write from their heart maps. (See Chapter 4 for more about reflecting on, sharing, and writing from heart maps.)

A word about making heart maps with our youngest writers

The first time I introduced heart mapping to kindergarten children was right before lunch. As a result, their heart maps were filled with drawings of sandwiches, chips, and ice cream! My advice is to wait until after lunch or snack time to introduce heart mapping to your youngest writers.

Like very young children's writing, their heart maps may consist mostly of drawing at first and then progressively include more writing in first and second grades. Some kindergartners and first graders, especially those who have written consistently in writing workshop and feel comfortable with writing letters and using invented spelling, may write and not draw any pictures at all on their heart maps.

Since very young children sometimes don't remember everything they draw or write, have a one-on-one conference with a child soon after she creates a heart map and write what she says on a sticky note to affix to the back of her heart map (I never write directly on students' heart maps) to help jog her memory later on. You can also encourage children to add letters or words to describe their pictures as they're creating their heart maps or at a later time.

When children finish heart mapping, give them ample time to share and talk with a writing partner, in small groups, or with the whole class. Just as in a writing workshop share, children can ask questions and make positive comments about each other's heart maps. During share time, or in a minilesson, ask children to carefully look over their heart maps, choose a favorite part, and storytell that part to a partner. Telling stories from their heart maps allows children to rehearse for writing, and speaking their stories out loud lets them

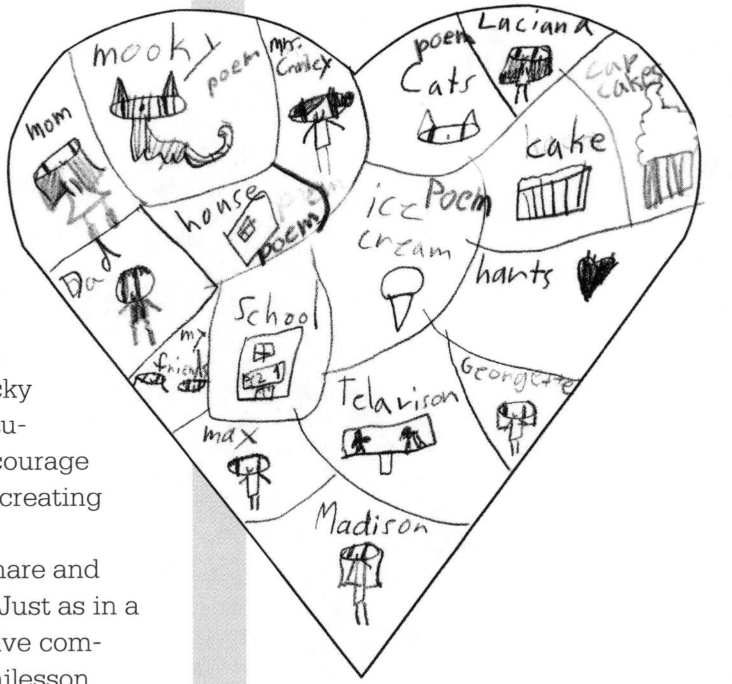

Figure 2.4 Anna was a confident first-grade writer, filling her map with pictures and labels.

fill in details to a partner. Children can choose another entry from their heart maps to tell and write about over the course of a week or a few weeks. Here are some other ways children can write from their heart maps:

- Ask them to point to more items on their heart maps that they might write a story, poem, or nonfiction piece about.
- Ask children to share any feelings that came up as they mapped their hearts. Suggest that they write down those feelings and what on their heart maps made them feel this way.

Young children can create heart maps on the covers of their writing folders to inspire ideas for writing, or you can display their heart maps on the walls (at

Figure 2.5 My son, Leo, made this heart map when he was in kindergarten. I love how he drew two diamonds next to his mom and dad because *our love is as strong as diamonds.*

eye level so kids can walk up to them to see and point to favorite words or drawings) to generate writing ideas.

Diane Sullivan, a teacher in Massachusetts, describes the elaborate and artistic process of her primary students painting heart maps with watercolor:

> Heart maps are a tradition in our class. Each year we spend time talking about how writers write about people and places and things that are close to their hearts. The children begin drawing and writing their ideas on large oak tag paper using pencil. Next, the pencil lines are covered with black [permanent marker]. Crayon comes next, followed by bright, concentrated watercolor applied with thick brushes. The paintings are then dried, pressed (they'll curl up), and mounted on black construction paper. The whole process takes several weeks. Year after year, the children enjoy making them and we get to know each other better in the process.

See the examples in Figures 2.8 through 2.15.

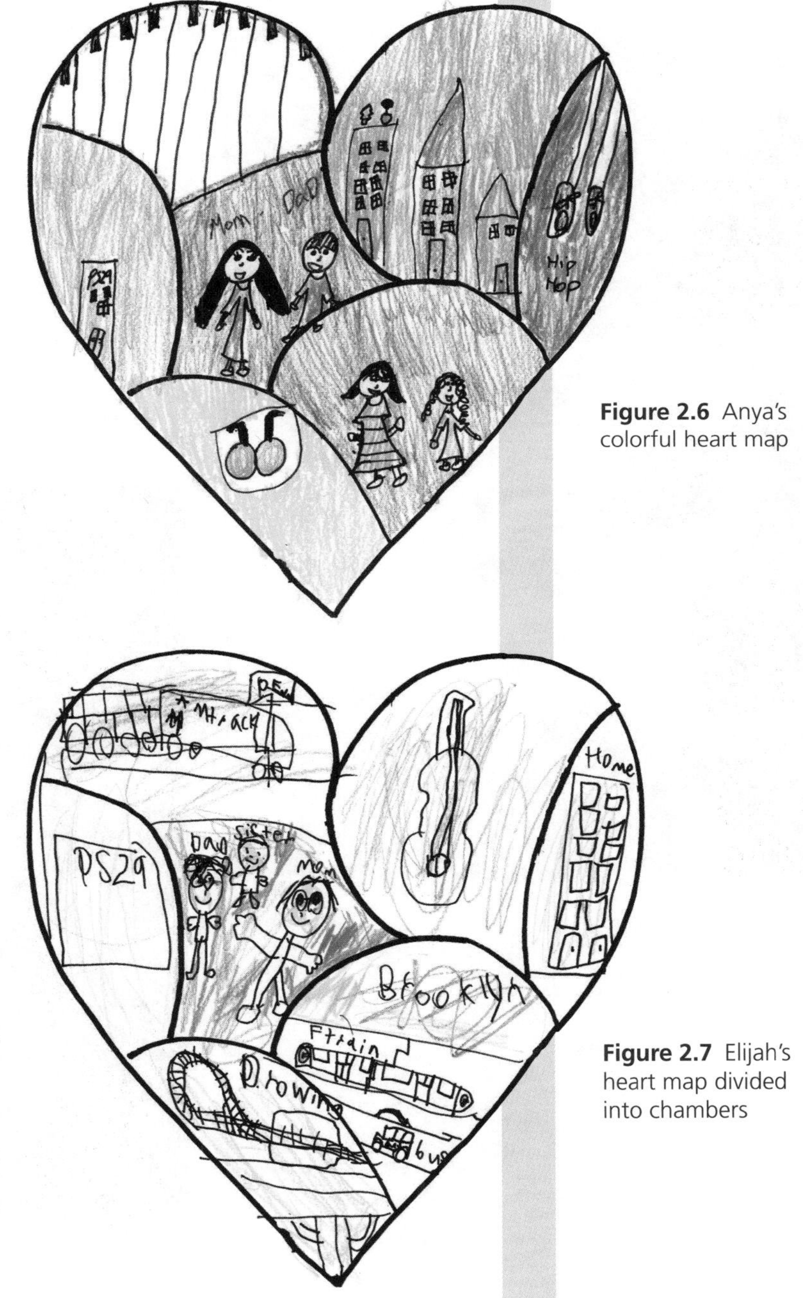

Figure 2.6 Anya's colorful heart map

Figure 2.7 Elijah's heart map divided into chambers

Figure 2.8
Eli drafting his heart map

Figure 2.9
Pastels for coloring heart maps

Figure 2.10
Eli painting his heart map

Figure 2.11 Watercolor and brushes for painting heart maps

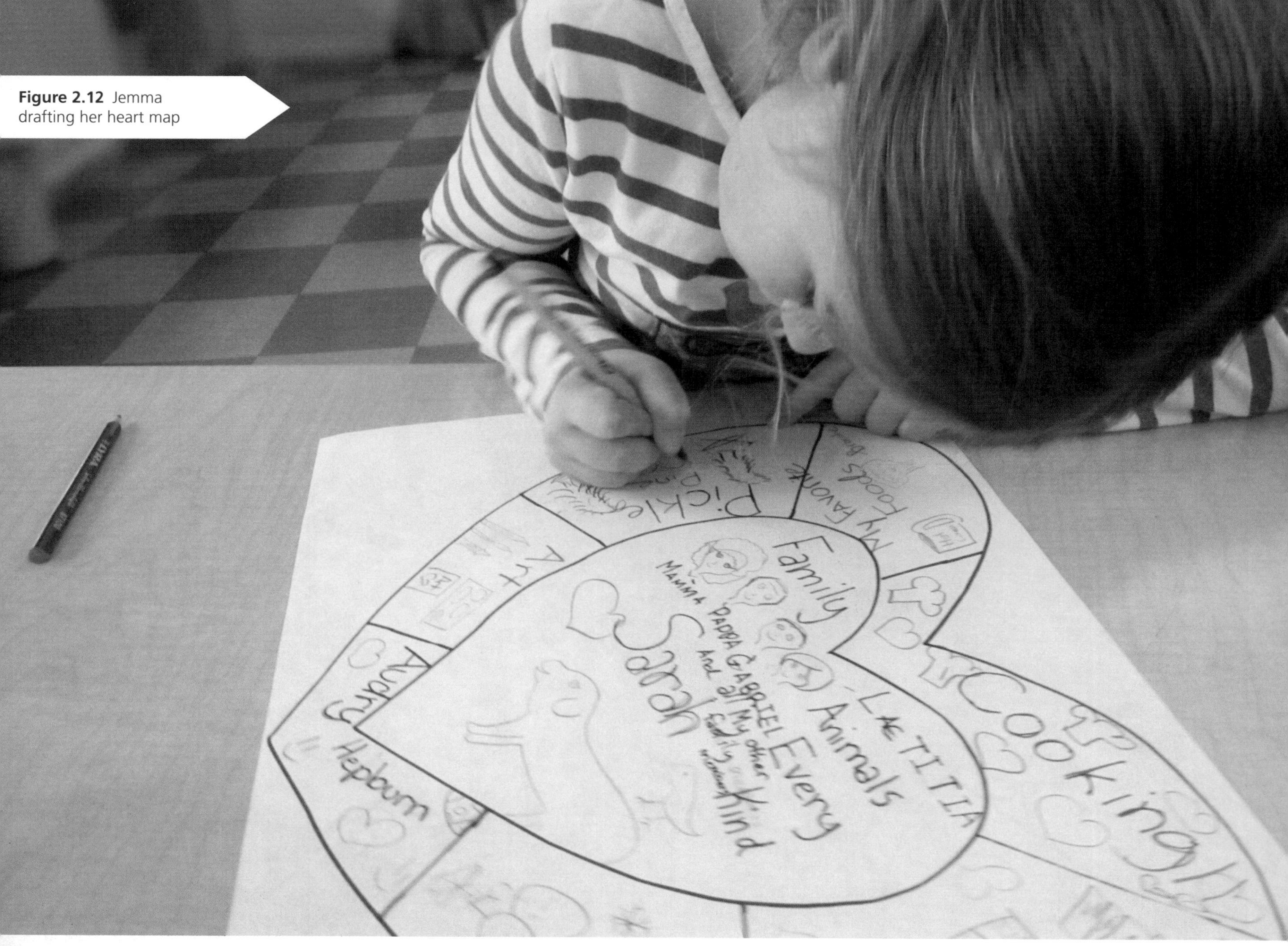

Figure 2.12 Jemma drafting her heart map

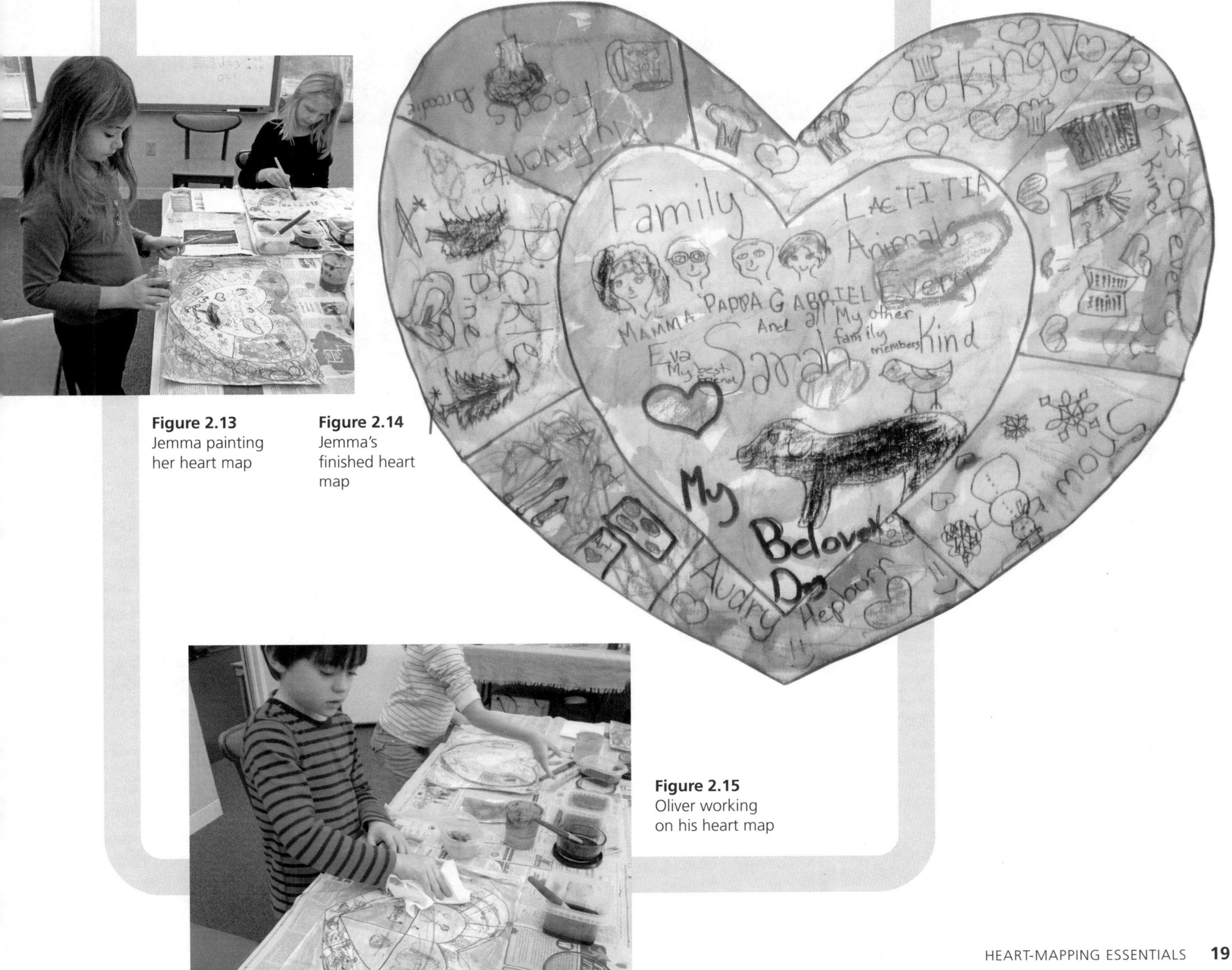

Figure 2.13 Jemma painting her heart map

Figure 2.14 Jemma's finished heart map

Figure 2.15 Oliver working on his heart map

3

SECTION TWO

The Heart of the Matter

Twenty Heart Maps to Inspire and Engage Writers

Let your heart choose what to pay attention to and stick with it. Bring it close with details for yourself and your readers.

—Robert Bly

Heart of the matter; speak from one's *heart*; put your *heart* into it; *heart*warming; straight from the *heart*; follow your *heart*; *heart* of gold; "Put a Little Love in Your *Heart*" . . .

The word *heart* is at the core of countless everyday expressions, poems, songs, and stories. The heart is, of course, the actual muscular organ that pumps our blood, but over time the word has come to represent something beyond: *love*; *what's essential*; *the innermost part of something.*

Writers love to unfold the meaning of words and peel back their history, and so I've unpacked the word *heart* and learned that it originated from the Latin *cor* and was then modified by the French into *cour*. It's fascinating to look at all the words that have *heart* or *cour* at their center:

courage (you must have *heart* to be courageous)

encourage (to give someone *heart* to keep going)

core (the *heart* of something, like the center of the planet)

discourage (to set apart someone's *heart* in a situation)

When I introduced heart mapping years ago, I started with just one kind of heart map, on which writers wrote about what they loved and what they had stored in their hearts. But just as there are hundreds of songs and poems that use the word and idea of *heart*, there are countless possibilities for heart maps. Revisiting heart mapping throughout the year doesn't mean students create the same heart map over and over again. I've mapped my heart dozens of times, and each time I discover new writing possibilities.

This chapter offers twenty different kinds of heart maps for you and your students to try. Each of the twenty heart maps focuses on a different topic or theme and invites students to dive deep in finding meaning and writing in multiple ways. Some of the heart map themes correspond to various genres in Lucy Calkins' writing Units of Study. Find a heart map that speaks to you and your classroom community or matches the kind of writing genre your classroom is engaged in. Introduce one kind of heart map to the whole class, or make heart map templates available to writers during independent writing time.

Each heart map section follows the same six-point structure:

1. An **introduction** to the type of heart map
2. A **"Try This"** section with instructions, tips for getting started, and how you might use the heart map template with your students
3. A **heart map template** accompanied by questions and ideas for writing and drawing (a printable heart map template can be found in the accompanying online resources)
4. **Writing ideas** for multiple genres
5. Student heart map **examples** or an example from me
6. **Mentor texts** to inspire writing from heart maps.

Just like when you turn a kaleidoscope and the shapes arrange themselves into different but similar patterns of light, these twenty heart maps overlap and complement one another and will inspire multiple writing genres. For detailed and practical how-to tips for heart mapping, see Chapter 2.

The companion online resources contain reproducible versions of each of the heart map templates, in black and white or color, that can be copied for students' use. Students can draw and write directly on each printable heart map and use the multiple questions and suggestions printed on the right-hand side to inspire as they map their hearts.

To access the online resources, visit **http://hein.pub /HeartMaps**. Enter your email address and password (or click "Create a New Account" to set up an account). Once you have logged in, enter keycode **HRTMPS** and click "Register".

Materials Needed

Essentials for making heart maps:

heart map template on 8½-by-11-inch paper

pencils, pens, crayons, thin markers, thin permanent markers, and watercolors

Possible additional materials:

copies of photographs, souvenirs, letters, or other artifacts to glue on heart maps

scissors for cutting out images from magazines or newspapers

watercolor brushes, if students will be painting their heart maps

glue, if students will be making collages with pictures, letters, or photos or gluing the maps in their writers' notebooks

If you're not using one of the heart map templates, writers can make their own heart maps with the following materials:

drawing or regular 8½-by-11-inch paper if they'll be taping their hearts into their writers' notebooks

12-by-18-inch white construction paper if you'll be displaying the maps on the wall

Heart-Mapping Design: Ideas and Questions

How students design their heart maps can convey meaning as well as the content they choose to write. Here are some design suggestions and questions that students might consider when creating open-ended heart maps.

- If you're drawing your own heart map, think about what shape you want your heart to be. For example, you can create a valentine heart, symbolic heart, or anatomical heart. Be inventive. Your heart map can be in any shape you want as long as it corresponds to something important in your life.
- Do you want to place the most important person, memory, or thing at the center of your heart and then continue working outward to less significant things, or do you have another idea about positioning?
- Do the positions of the entries on your heart map correspond to their significance in your life?
- What size words will you use? Do words written larger communicate more significant events and smaller words less important ones?
- What can you place outside around the edges that might be less important to you?
- Do you want to include drawing and writing?
- Do you want to use color? How do different colors represent particular feelings?
- Do you want to draw more than one heart—for example, good and bad; happy and sad; secret and open—and include different things inside each heart?
- You can also create a heart map collage by copying photos, letters, or other artifacts and gluing them onto your map.
- Do you want to include a map key or legend?

In addition to the previous suggestions, I hope writers will invent their own ways of exploring heart maps, and that heart mapping will support writers in finding life topics that will surprise them, amaze them, and help them discover new doorways into themselves and the world of writing.

What is a map key or legend?

Maps sometimes use symbols, numbers, pictures, or colors to give additional information. A map key or legend explains what those symbols, numbers, pictures, or colors mean. Map keys are usually boxes in the corner of a map, and the information in the key is important to understanding the map. You might consider encouraging students to create keys or legends for their own maps!

1

Blank Canvas Heart Map

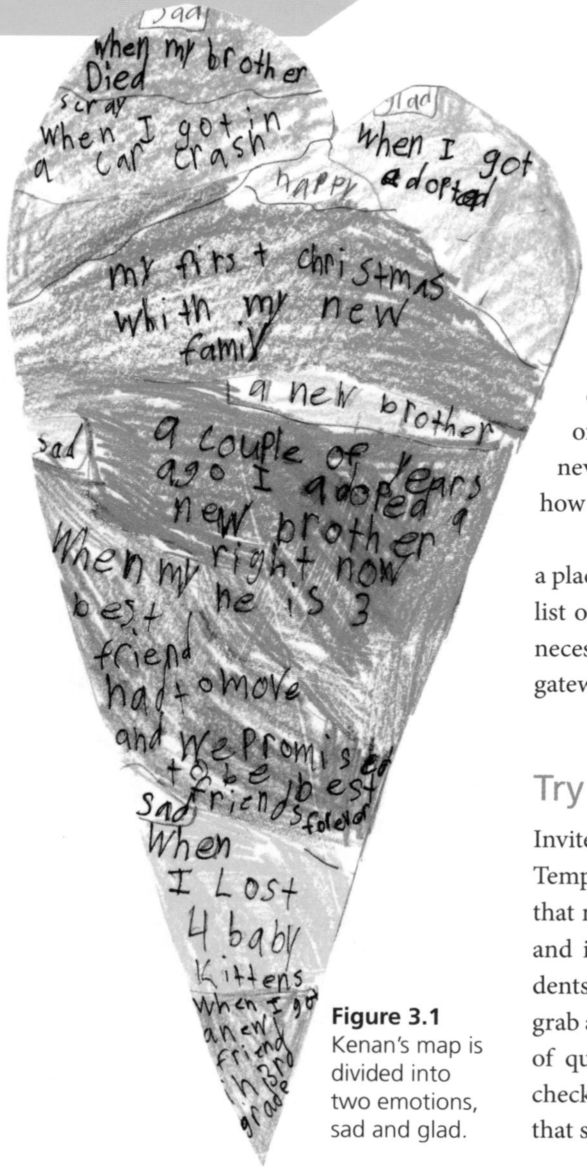

Figure 3.1 Kenan's map is divided into two emotions, sad and glad.

Introduction

When I paint, I stand in front of my canvas and my heart beats with the anticipation of how I'm going to fill it with color and light. An empty canvas means possibilities and a little bit of mystery. As I dip my brush into the paint, I never know exactly how the painting will turn out, how the light will change, what the colors will be.

This first heart map is like a blank canvas. It's a place to explore, play, and meander. I've included a list of possibilities as well as questions that are not necessarily meant to be answered, but to serve as gateways for mapping your heart.

Try This

Invite writers to use the Blank Canvas Heart Map Template to map things, people, and experiences that matter to them. This heart map is open-ended and invites writers to play and explore. Your students' hearts might be so full that they may want to grab a larger piece of paper to fit everything. The list of questions on the heart map template is not a checklist. Writers can read through and find ideas that speak to them.

Writing Ideas

This heart map supports writing in all genres. Students can follow these steps to get started:

1. Choose one item on your heart map that catches your heart and write it down in a writer's notebook or on a separate sheet of paper.

Figure 3.2 Nico's heart map is a jigsaw puzzle with puzzle pieces for categories such as *Journeys, Dreams and Comforts*, and so on.

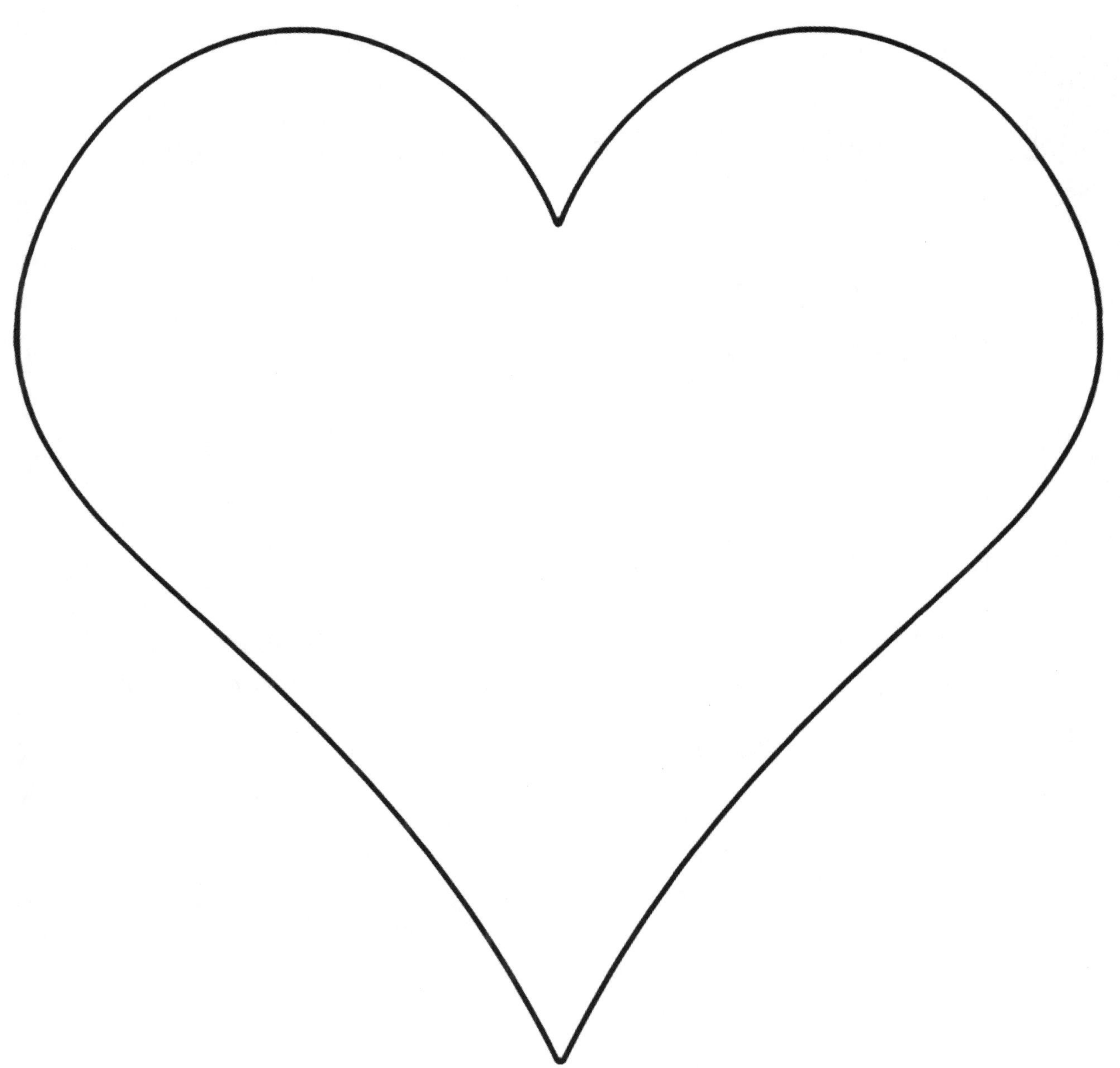

Blank Canvas Heart Map Template

- What memories and feelings have you stored in your heart?
- What memories, people, and experiences have made you who you are today?
- What people have been important to you?
- What places have been important to you, and what memories do these places hold for you?
- What are some experiences or central events that you will never forget?
- What happy or sad memories do you have?
- What makes your heart sing?
- What secrets have you kept in your heart? (You don't have to share the secret; find a metaphor to explain it instead.)
- What small things or objects are important to you—for example, a tree in your backyard, a trophy, a stuffed animal?
- What do you want to tell others about yourself?
- What are the important things about your
  - ☐ feelings?
  - ☐ talents?
  - ☐ likes and dislikes?
  - ☐ challenges?
- What is unique about you?

Here are some additional ideas to consider when heart mapping:

- your future
- your life history
- your wishes and dreams
- an idea you've had
- what you are grateful for.

Name: ______________________

____

Date: ______________________

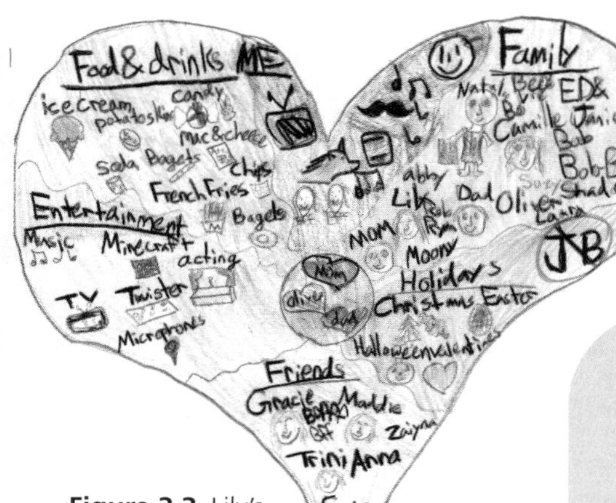

Figure 3.3 Lily's Blank Canvas heart map is filled with what she loves.

2. Ask yourself, "What genre does this topic beg to be written in? Poem; personal narrative; essay; memoir . . . ?"
3. Begin exploring the topic by freewriting any thoughts, images, and feelings.
4. Think about painting the pictures in your mind with words as you write.
5. Periodically, stop and reread and layer sensory details into your writing.

Mentor Texts

- Bruce, Mary. "'One Today': Full Text of Richard Blanco Inaugural Poem." ABC News. http://abcnews.go.com/Politics/today-richard-blanco-poem-read-barack-obama-inauguration/story?id=18274653. (4+)
- Blanco, Richard. 2015. *One Today*. New York: Little Brown Books for Young Readers. (Preschool–3)
- Cummings, E. E. 2014. *I Carry Your Heart with Me*. Petaluma, CA: Cameron. (Preschool–K)
- Dotlich, Rebecca Kai. 2016. *The Knowing Book*. Honesdale, PA: Boyds Mills. (K+)
- Johnson, Georgia Douglas. 1918. "The Heart of a Woman" in *The Heart of a Woman and Other Poems*. Boston: The Cornhill Company. (8)
- Kalman, Maira. 2009. *The Principles of Uncertainty*. New York: Penguin Books. (10+)
- Laux, Dorianne. 2000. "Heart" in *Smoke*. Rochester, NY: BOA Editions, Ltd. (9+)
- Strand, Mark. 2007. "The Coming of Light." In *New Selected Poems*. New York: Alfred A. Knopf. (9+)
- Witek, Jo. 2014. *In My Heart: A Book of Feelings*. New York: Harry N. Abrams. (Preschool–1)

2

My Writer's Heart Map

Introduction

In every writer's heart, there are roads that have led us to our writing path: a first notebook; a beloved bedtime story; a teacher who praised our words. There are details from memories, people we've loved, and places we've lived paving the paths to our stories, poems, and nonfiction.

In the center of my heart map I drew two images (see Figure 3.5). First, my three sisters, my mother, and my father sitting around a table, with happy tears streaming from my mother's eyes as I read a birthday poem aloud to her. When I was a girl, I wrote birthday poems for all my relatives, which I sometimes read aloud at family gatherings. The other image is the lock-and-key diary my parents gave me. There I discovered I could confide how I truly felt; it became the place I kept my secrets and innermost feelings.

I also wrote and drew other inspirations on my heart map: favorite writers; saved words from beloved poems and books; the details of places I've lived that have found a place in my writing.

Try This

Writers can use the My Writer's Heart Map Template to draw and write about themselves as writers and to express their early writing memories, inspirations, and ideas about writing.

My Writer's Heart maps help me get to know writers better by learning who they are as writers: about their feelings towards writing; what they like, and don't like, about writing, what they

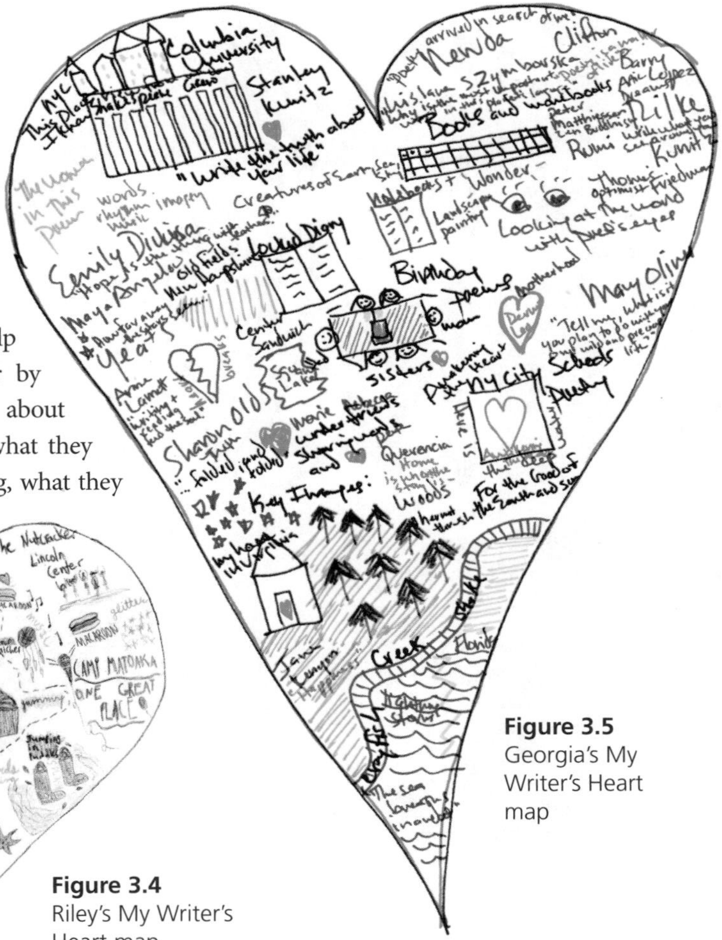

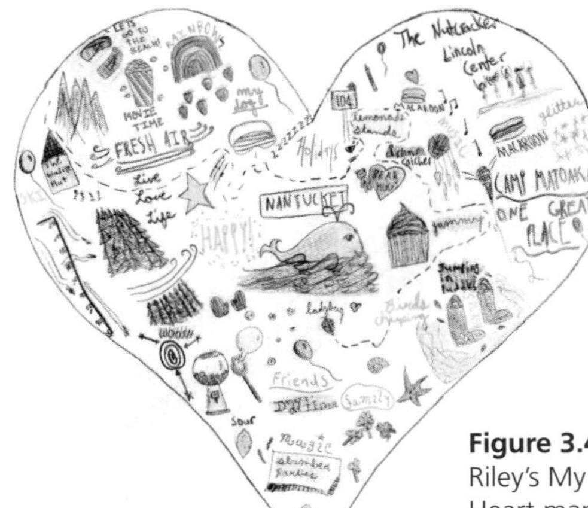

Figure 3.4
Riley's My Writer's Heart map

Figure 3.5
Georgia's My Writer's Heart map

My Writer's Heart Map Template

In the center of your heart you could include any of the following:

- early writing memories including how you got started writing
- how you feel about yourself as a writer
- the kind of writer you are (for example, a poet, a nonfiction writer, etc.).

Other ideas for a My Writer's Heart map:

- favorite writers
- favorite books and poems that have sparked your writing
- what inspires you to write
- favorite place to write
- places that inspire you to write
- how you get your writing ideas
- types of writing you like (for example, poetry, fiction, etc.)
- favorite words you have used in your writing
- a sample of your best writing
- favorite writing tools (pencil, special colored pen, notebook, etc.).

Name: ______________________

____

Date: ______________________

struggle with, and so on, all of which guides me in my conferences and minilessons.

You might suggest that students create two My Writer's Heart maps: one at the beginning of the school year and a second one toward the end of the year. They can then compare their two heart maps to see how they've grown and changed as writers.

Be sure to build in time for rereading, reflecting, and sharing. Here are some questions and ideas that might generate conversation and inspire more extended pieces of writing:

- What did I discover about myself when I mapped my writer's heart?
- What surprised me when I created my writer's heart?
- Is there one thing on my heart map that is the most important that I could expand upon by writing more?

Writing Ideas

This heart map works best to support writing in personal narrative, memoir, poem, or essay. Here are some ideas students could try:

- Write a personal narrative, essay, or memoir about yourself as a writer. Gather details from your heart map, such as how you got started writing, how you feel about yourself as a writer, how you get writing ideas, and places that inspire you to write, to include in your essay or personal narrative.

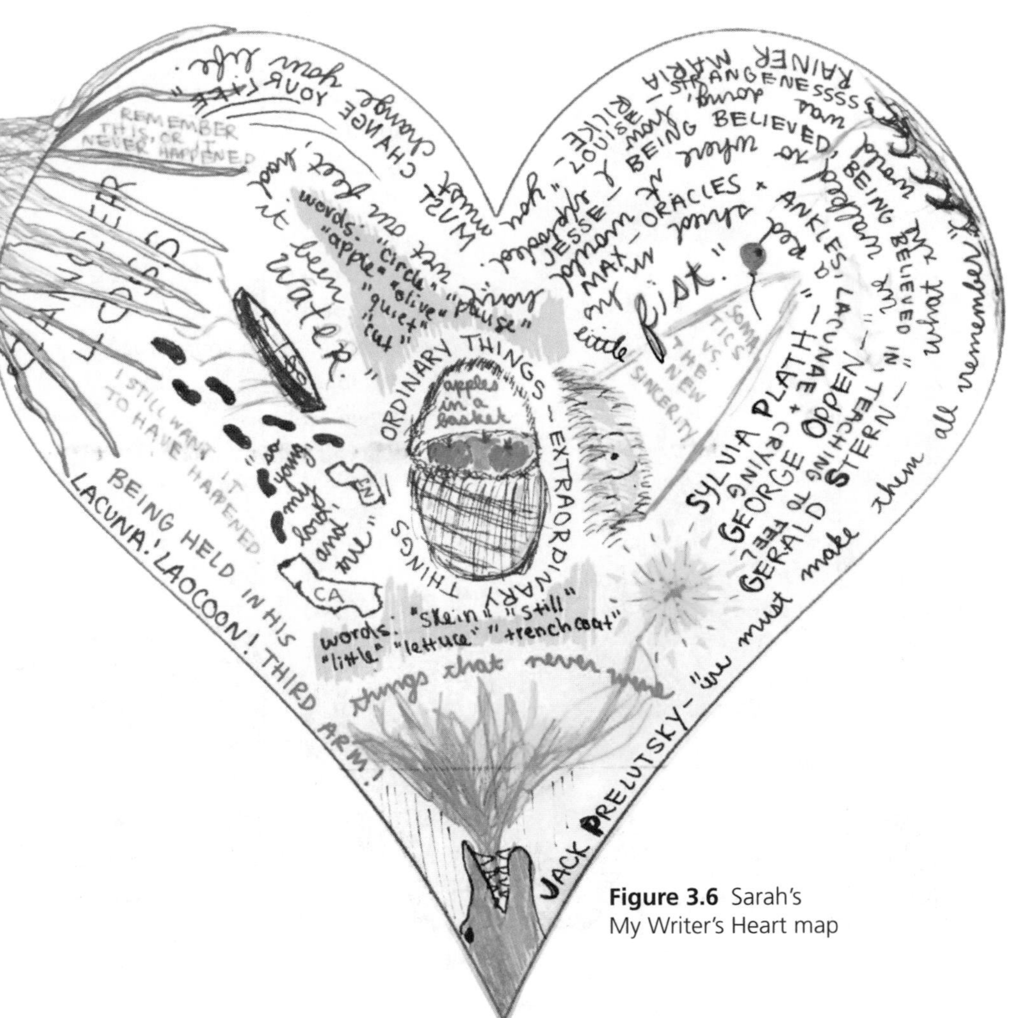

Figure 3.6 Sarah's My Writer's Heart map

- Choose one entry on your heart map that inspires you and write a poem. Franny chose *the great horned owl* from her heart map (see Figure 3.10) and wrote this poem:

Wise Eyes

Bright wise eyes
staring down
in the thick
blue sky.
You fly
wings flap
without sound.
The low *whoos*
rumble deep in your throat.
Whoo whoo
Whoo whoo
You call out to the sky.

- Write a poem about yourself as a writer or your writing process. Include details from your heart map such as where you like to write, what tools you like to write with, and what you love or what is difficult about writing.

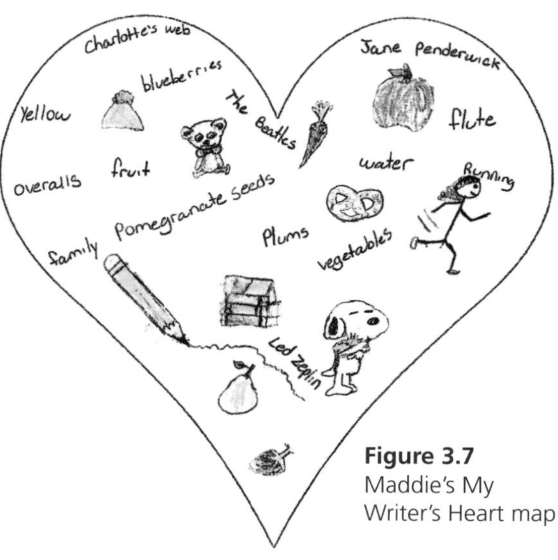

Figure 3.7 Maddie's My Writer's Heart map

Figure 3.8 Merr's variation of a My Writer's Heart map in the shape of a pencil

Mentor Texts

- Alifirenka, Caitlin, and Martin Ganda. 2015. *I Will Always Write Back: How One Letter Changed Two Lives*. With Liz Welch. New York: Little, Brown Books for Young Readers. (7+)
- Bram, Elizabeth. 2015. *Rufus the Writer*. New York: Schwartz and Wade. (Preschool–3)
- Ehrlich, Amy, ed. 2012. *When I Was Your Age: Original Stories About Growing Up, Volumes I and II*. Somerville, MA: Candlewick. (4–7)
- Fritz, Jean. 1990. *Hey World, Here I Am!* New York: Harper Trophy Books. (3–7)
- Janeczko, Paul. 1990. *The Place My Words Are Looking For: What Poets Say About and Through Their Work*. New York: Simon and Schuster. (4–7)
- MacLachlan, Patricia. 2006. *Word After Word After Word*. New York: Puffin Books. (1–4)
- Moss, Marissa. 2012. *Amelia Writes Again*. New York: Simon and Schuster/Paula Wiseman Books. (2–5)
- Pilkey, Dav. 2008. "On Writing." In *Guys Write for Guys Read: Boys' Favorite Authors Write About Being Boys*, by Jon Scieszka, 130–32. New York: Viking Books for Young Readers. (5+)

Figure 3.9 Jonah's My Writer's Heart map with key

- Salisbury, Graham. 1994. "A Leaf on the Sea." *The ALAN Review* 22 (1). https://scholar.lib.vt.edu/ejournals/ALAN/fall94/Salisbury.html. (7–12)
- Smothers, Ethel Footman. 2003. *The Hard-Times Jar*. New York: Farrar Straus and Giroux. (Preschool–3)
- Spinelli, Eileen. 2008. *The Best Story*. New York: Dial Books for Young Readers. (1–3)
- Tuck, Pamela M. 2013. *As Fast as Words Could Fly*. New York: Lee and Low Books. (2–5)
- Wong, Janet. 2002. *You Have to Write*. New York: Margaret K. McElderry Books. (3–7)
- Woodson, Jacqueline. 2014. *Brown Girl Dreaming*. New York: Nancy Paulsen Books. (5+)

Poetry

- Collins, Billy. 1996. "Introduction to Poetry." In *The Apple That Astonished Paris*. Fayetteville: University of Arkansas Press. (6+)

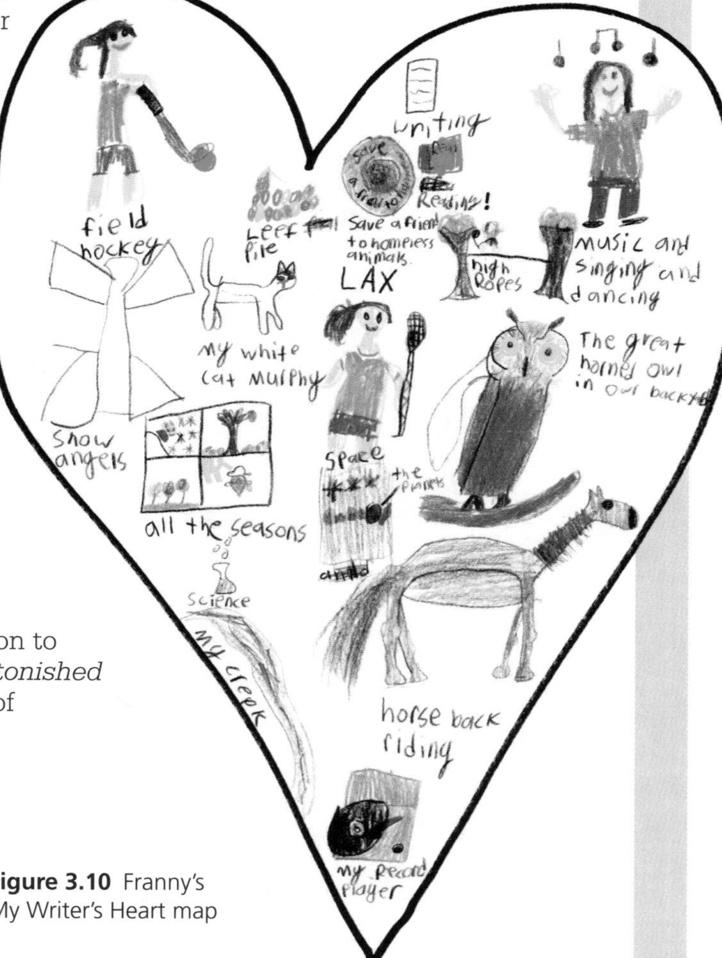

Figure 3.10 Franny's My Writer's Heart map

- Herrera, Juan Felipe. 2008. "Let Me Tell You What a Poem Brings." In *Half of the World in Light: New and Selected Poems*. Tucson: University of Arizona Press. (7+)
- Koriyama, Naoshi. 1957. "Unfolding Bud." *Christian Science Monitor*, July 13. (2+)
- McEwan, Mira. 2007. "Words That Make My Stomach Plummet." In *Ecstatic*. Selden, NY: Allbook Books. (8+)
- Moffitt, John. 1997. "To Look at Any Thing." In *Reflections on a Gift of a Watermelon Pickle . . . and Other Modern Verse*, 2d edition, edited by Stephen Dunning, Edward Lueders, and Hugh Smith. Boston: Addison Wesley. (1+)
- Mojgani, Anis. 2010. "Shake the Dust." (Video recording). To Write Love on Her Arms. https://vimeo.com/8746269. (7+)
- Nye, Naomi Shihab. 1994. "Valentine for Earnest Mann." In *Red Suitcase*, 70. Rochester, NY: BOA Editions. (2+)
- Schultz, Philip. 2007. "What I Like and Don't Like." In *Failure*. San Diego: Harcourt. (9+)

My Reader's Heart Map

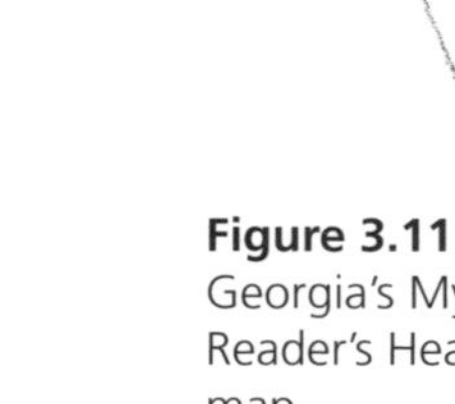

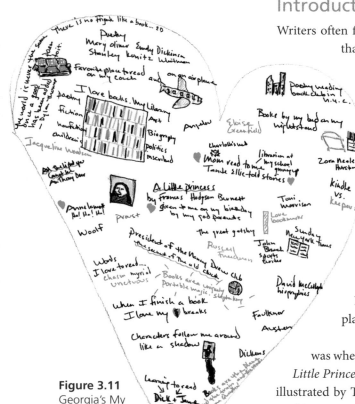

Figure 3.11 Georgia's My Reader's Heart map

Introduction

Writers often form a deep friendship with reading that begins at an early age. One highlight of my early reading life was becoming president of the Nancy Drew Club when I was in sixth grade. My obsession with Nancy Drew books began with my mother's old editions. *The Secret of the Old Clock* and *The Mystery at Lilac Inn* were two of my favorites, and I then moved on to collecting my own. During our Nancy Drew Club meetings, my friends and I shared Nancy Drew's sleuthing secrets and planned which books to read next.

The second early reading memory was when my godmother gave me a copy of *A Little Princess*, by Frances Hodgson Burnett, and illustrated by Tasha Tudor, as a birthday present. I read it over and over again. It still sits on my bookshelf today, tattered and well loved. See Figure 3.11 for my own My Reader's Heart map.

Try This

Students can use the book-like My Reader's Heart Map Template to map themselves as readers: their reading lives, reading memories, and favorite books and authors. Invite students to create a My Reader's Heart map at the very beginning of the school year and then again at the end. After they map their readers' hearts, build in time for reflection and sharing. Readers will most likely discover books and authors that they love and have in common, and they might possibly form reading clubs based on their heart-mapping discoveries. Later in the year, after they create their second My Reader's Heart map, they can reflect on and share how they've grown and changed as readers.

The following are some questions and ideas students can ask themselves that might inspire writing and discussion after heart mapping:

- What did I discover about myself when I mapped my reader's heart?
- What surprised me when I created my reader's heart?
- Is there one thing on my heart map that seems the most important that I could expand upon and write more about?

My Reader's Heart Map Template

Start in the center of your heart map by describing yourself as a reader and/or how you feel about reading. Here are some ideas for mapping your reader's heart:

- favorite authors
- favorite books or poems and why you like them
- memorable lines, phrases, or words from books you've read
- favorite characters and why they're your favorite
- favorite place to read
- memories of reading
- memories of being read to
- books or characters that have influenced your life
- special books that were given to you as gifts
- favorite types of books you like to read (for example, poetry, dystopia novels, etc.)
- reading habits (reading late at night, reading two books at once, etc.).

Alternatively, you could focus on one reading experience that is important to you:

- In the center of your heart map, write what you love about a book, a poem, or some other text.
- What feelings did you have as you read the book or poem? Can you identify where and why the writing made you feel this way?
- How has the book, poem, or text personally affected you or changed you in some way?

Name: ______________________

____

Date: ______________________

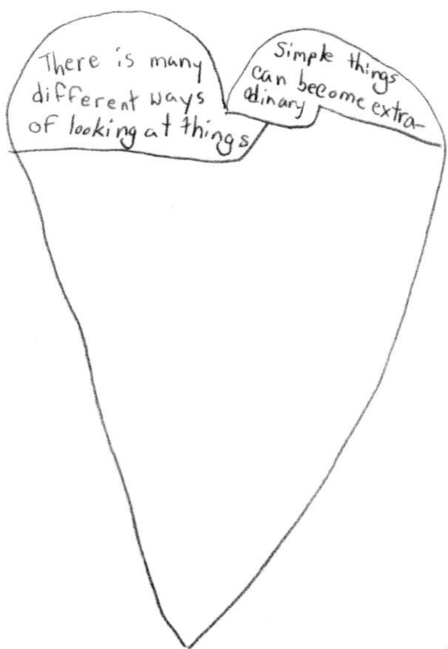

Figure 3.12 Ben read *All the Small Poems and Fourteen More*, by Valerie Worth, and described the essence of Worth's poems in his heart map: "There [are] many different ways of looking at things" and "Simple things can become extraordinary."

Writing Ideas

This heart map works best to support writing personal narrative, memoir, poem, essay, fiction, or photojournalism. Offer students one or more of these ideas:

- Write a personal narrative, essay, or memoir about yourself as a reader. Gather details from your reader's heart, such as what you discovered about yourself as a reader, the kind of reader you are, and your earlier memories of reading and being read to, to include in your writing.
- Write a poem about you as a reader, what you love or dislike about reading, or a favorite book or poem.
- If you keep a reader's notebook, tape your heart map in your notebook and then write entries from your reader's heart map.
- Create a photojournalism text by taking photos (or asking a teacher to take photos) of kids reading in your school or class and then interviewing them briefly about their reading lives and writing their words beneath your photos. You might ask them the same questions as you asked for your My Reader's Heart map.
- Explore the imaginative side of your reading life and write a fiction story based on your reader's heart map.

Mentor Texts

- Adams, Jen. 2012. *The Books They Gave Me: True Stories of Life, Love, and Lit*. New York: Simon and Schuster. (10+)
- Bunting, Eve. 1989. *The Wednesday Surprise*. Boston: HMH Books for Young Readers. (Preschool–3)
- Hest, Amy. 2007. *Mr. George Baker*. New York: Reading Rainbow Books. (K–3)
- ———. 2012. *The Reader*. Las Vegas, NV: Amazon Publishing. (K–2)
- Hoff, Dawn. 2015. "26 Inspiring Poems About the Joys and Importance of Books and Reading." *Bookkidsblog*, April 10. https://bookkidsblog.wordpress.com/2015/04/10/26-inspiring-poems-about-the-joys-and-importance-of-books-and-reading/. (K+)
- Hoffman, Mary. 1991. *Amazing Grace*. New York: Dial Books. (Preschool–3)
- Hopkins, Lee Bennett. 2004. *Wonderful Words: Poems About Reading, Writing, Speaking, and Listening*. New York: Simon and Schuster Books for Young Readers. (1–6)

- ———. 2015. *Jumping Off Library Shelves: A Book of Poems*. Honesdale, PA: WordSong. (K+)
- Jones, Patrick. 2008. "Wrestling with Reading." In *Guys Write for Guys Read: Boys' Favorite Authors Write About Being Boys*, edited by Jon Scieszka, 127–29. New York: Viking Books for Young Readers. (5+)
- Kousky, Vern. 2015. *Otto the Owl Who Loved Poetry*. New York: Nancy Paulsen Books. (K–3)
- Lewis, J. Patrick. 2005. *Please Bury Me in the Library*. Boston: HMH Books for Young Readers. (Preschool–3)
- Makkai, Rebecca. 2012. *The Borrower*. New York: Penguin Books. (10+)
- McQuinn, Anna. 2010. *Lola Loves Stories*. Watertown, MA: Charlesbridge. (Preschool–K)
- ———. 2012. *Lola Reads to Leo*. Watertown, MA: Charlesbridge. (Preschool–K)
- Nastasi, Alison. 2013. "12 Beautiful Poems for Book Lovers." *Flavorwire*, February 24. flavorwire.com. (2+)
- Smothers, Ethel Footman. 2003. *The Hard-Times Jar*. New York: Farrar Straus and Giroux. (Preschool–3)
- Woodson, Jacqueline. 2014. "reading." In *Brown Girl Dreaming*, 226. New York: Nancy Paulsen Books. (5+)
- Zagarenski, Pamela. 2015. *The Whisper*. Boston: HMH Books for Young Readers. (Preschool–3)

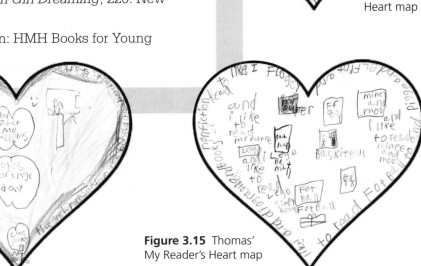

Figure 3.14 Uriel's My Reader's Heart map

Figure 3.13 Lincoln's My Reader's Heart map

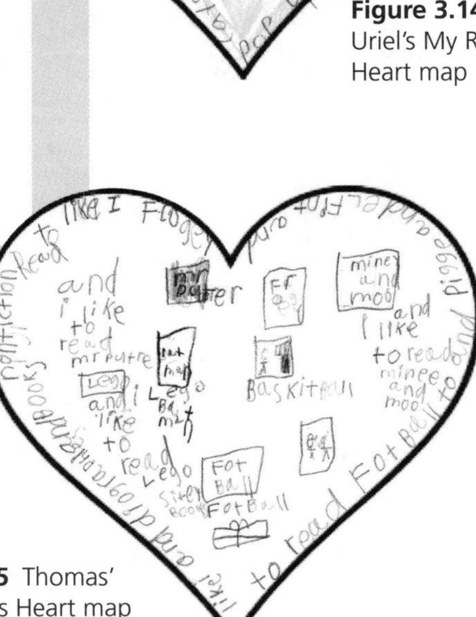

Figure 3.15 Thomas' My Reader's Heart map

4

Small Moment Heart Maps

Introduction

A small moment is a freeze-frame instant stored in our memories that we then stretch out into a longer story. Small moments are like snowflakes — tiny and unique — and over time they accumulate to make a blanket of white.

Author Lee Martin (2015) writes:

> If I had it to do over again, I'd tell the younger writer I was [that] if he can't make something out of the small and intimate, he'll never be able to make anything out of something large and distant.

Here are a few examples of my small moments. As I write, I like to remember this wise writing advice: "The bigger the idea, the smaller you write."

- Not the entire two weeks of summer spent at my grandparents' house, but when my sisters and I played mah-jongg with my ninety-year-old grandmother every evening, hearing the clicking of the mah-jongg tiles — bamboos, characters, and circles — before my grandmother proclaimed her nightly win: *Mah-jongg!*
- Not all the years growing up in Alexandria, Virginia, but the icy, snow-packed igloo my sister and I built during the blizzard of '68 and how we pretended we were Inuit living inside, protected as the snow fell heavily outside.
- Not all twenty years of living in New York City, but the maple tree outside my apartment window — its first buds breaking open in March, bringing hope after a cold, long winter.

When I write personal narrative, poetry, or memoir, I stretch these small moments out and slow time down minute by minute. Then I ask myself, "What larger meaning do these small moments have?"

Try This

Small moment writing is often geared towards our youngest writers but focusing on small moments can be useful to writers of all ages. Writers can use one of two small moment heart map templates to map out small moment ideas from their hearts. The first is for brainstorming multiple small moment memories and stories. Invite writers to think of things that have happened to them—something true in their lives, an everyday event, memories, true stories from their lives—and draw and write those moments on the small hearts in Small Moment Heart Map Version 1.

The second, Small Moment Heart Map Version 2, is for mapping out one small moment in detail, zooming in and stretching out a small moment using sensory details.

Writing Ideas

This heart map works best to support small moment writing, personal narrative, and poetry. Provide students some prompts like the following.

If you completed the first type of small moment heart map:

- Read over all the entries from your map and select one that resonates for you emotionally, catches your heart, or gives you an image in your mind. You can then complete the second small moment heart map to zoom in on details and stretch the moment into a longer story. You can also begin by writing this entry, and as you write, include more sensory details.
- Look over the entries on your map and ask, "How might these entries connect with one another?" Is there a statement you could make to connect them? Then write about these connections.

If you completed the second type of small moment heart map:

- Read over the details on your heart map and decide where you might begin your story or poem. Then begin writing, weaving in heart map entries as you write.
- Try writing a poem from the sensory details on your heart map.

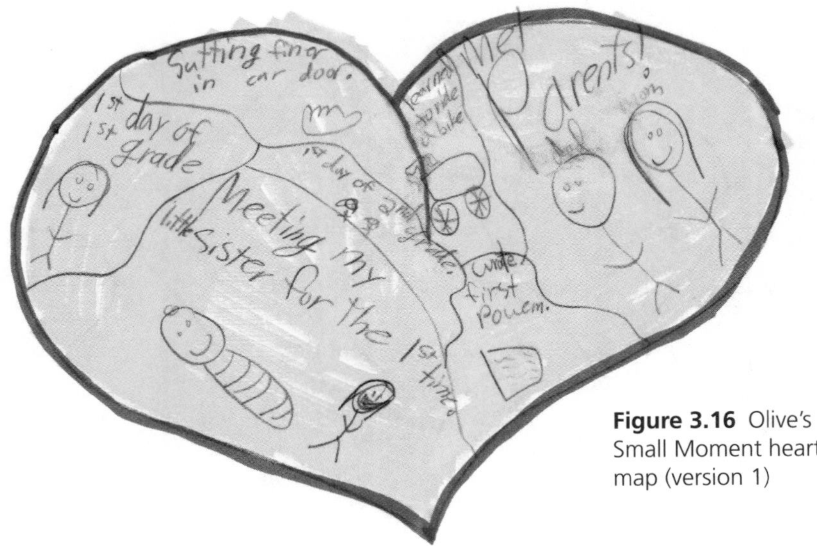

Figure 3.16 Olive's Small Moment heart map (version 1)

Small Moment Heart Map Template Version 1: Multiple Small Moments

Include some of the following:

- things that have happened to you
- something true in your life
- an every day event
- memories
- true stories from your life.

Name: ____________________

____

Date: ____________________

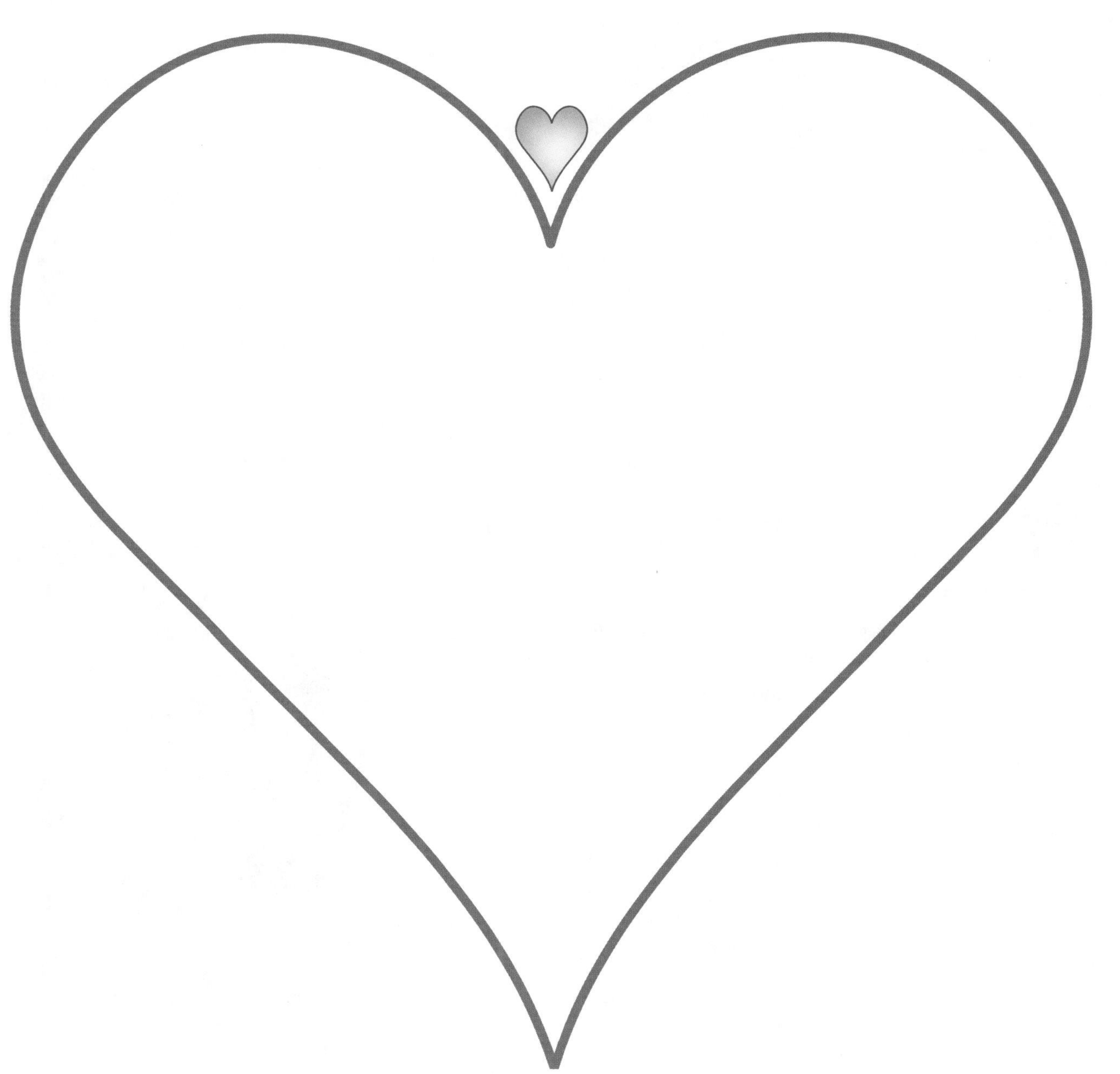

Small Moment Heart Map Template Version 2: A Focus on One Moment

Write the small moment in the center of your heart map and then explore questions and ideas such as these:

- Zoom in and stretch out your small moment using tiny details.
- Make a picture in your mind of the small moment and write the picture using your words.
- Describe sensory details such as what you hear (sounds and voices), what you see, or any memories of touch.
- What do you really want to say?
- Why is this small moment meaningful to you and how do you feel when you think of the small moment?

Name: ______________________

____

Date: ______________________

Mentor Texts

- Anastasia, Natasha. 2001. *I Love My Hair!* New York: Little, Brown Books for Young Readers. (Preschool–2)
- Aragon, Jane Chelsea. 1994. *Salt Hands*. New York: Puffin. (K–3)
- Bunting, Eve. 2001. *Jin Woo*. New York: Clarion Books. (Preschool–3)
- Cisneros, Sandra. 1997. *Hairs/Pelitos*. Decorah, IA: Dragonfly Books. (K–3)
- Crews, Donald. 1996. *Shortcut*. New York: Greenwillow Books. (Preschool–3)
- ———. 1998. *Bigmama's*. New York: Greenwillow Books. (Preschool–3)
- Garza, Carmen Lomas. 2005. *Family Pictures/Cuadros de familia*. San Francisco: Children's Book Press. (1+)
- Hoffman, Mary. 1991. *Amazing Grace*. New York: Dial Books. (Preschool–3)
- Pilkey, Dav. 1996. *The Paperboy*. New York: Orchard Books. (Preschool–3)
- Ray, Mary Lyn. 2005. *Red Rubber Boot Day*. New York: HMH Books for Young Readers. (Preschool–3)
- Schotter, Roni. 1999. *Nothing Ever Happens on 90th Street*. New York: Scholastic. (3–5)
- Spinelli, Eileen. 2001. *Night Shift Daddy*. New York: Scholastic. (Preschool–1)
- Willems, Mo. 2004. *Knuffle Bunny: A Cautionary Tale*. New York: Hyperion. (Preschool–K)

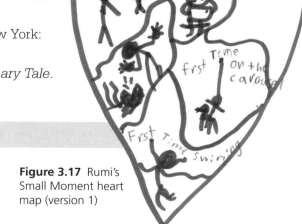

Figure 3.17 Rumi's Small Moment heart map (version 1)

5

First Time Heart Map

Introduction

Turning points are moments in our lives that change us, make us look at the world in a new way, and open our hearts. *First times* are examples of turning points that can inspire writing in many genres.

I remember the first time I went ice-skating with my Brownie troop. I wanted to get my skating badge to add to the collection sewn on my sash. As I skated around the rink, I felt like a bird flying free and light as the world spun around me. I loved the whoosh of cold air on my face and in my hair. That was my very first experience of what was to become seven years of ice-skating: getting up in the early-morning dark before school to practice; learning axels, salchows, and double flips; driving to regional competitions; and then becoming a professional skater and teaching figure skaters and hockey players how to skate when I was seventeen years old.

As I reflect on the significance of that first time now, I think of how all those years of skating taught me how to persevere and love something enough to spend hours, days, and years practicing. My love of ice-skating has transformed into my love of writing, as I sit at my desk day after day and year after year, spinning words instead of salchows and axels.

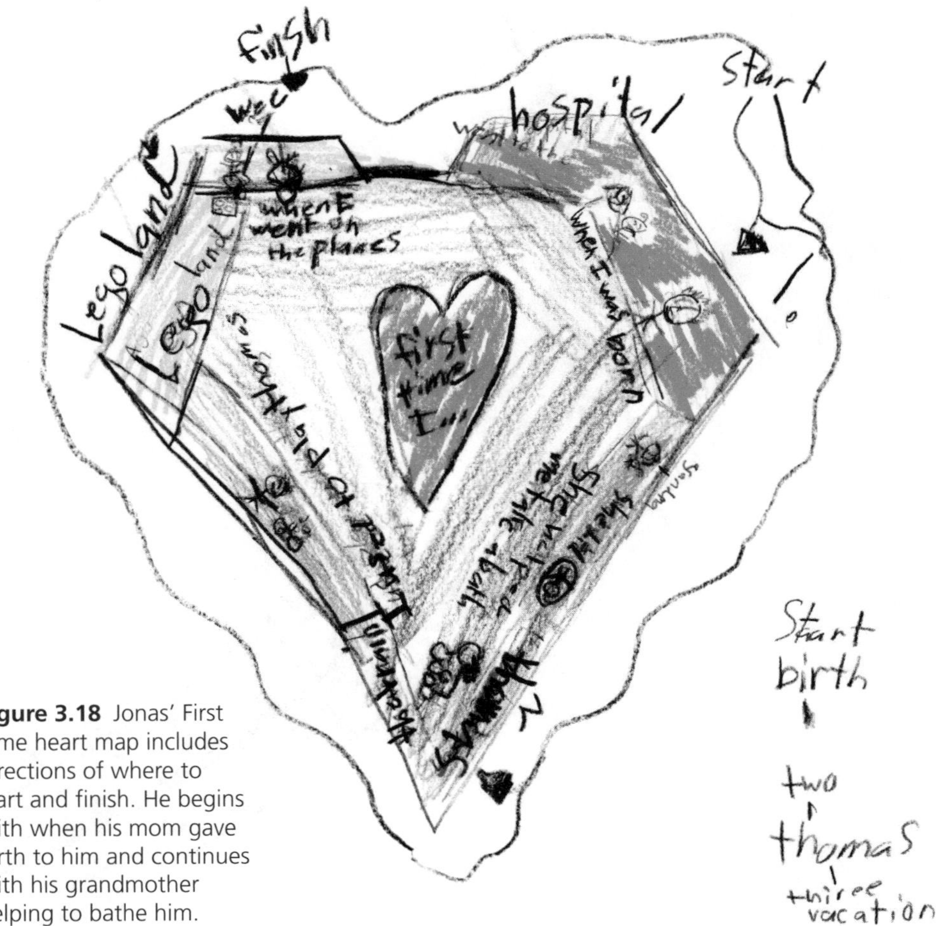

Figure 3.18 Jonas' First Time heart map includes directions of where to start and finish. He begins with when his mom gave birth to him and continues with his grandmother helping to bathe him.

First Time Heart Map Template

Here are some ideas that might inspire your First Time heart map:

The First Time You . . .

- saw the country or city or town where you now live
- went to a new school
- met your best friend
- saw your baby brother or sister
- played a sport you now play all the time
- got a pet
- realized something important about yourself
- won an award or a trophy
- went to the hospital
- read a book you love and have since read over and over again.

Name: ______________________

____

Date: ______________________

Try This

Writers can use the shiny First Time Heart Map Template frame to map out a self-portrait of meaningful first times—turning points in their lives, such as the first time they fell in love with something; did something that they now do daily; met a friend; laid eyes on a new sibling; a first memory; or the first time they realized something significant about themselves. As students map their hearts they might also add sensory details of their first times to paint a vivid picture.

Writing Ideas

The First Time heart map supports writing in personal narrative, essay, poem, and memoir. Give students some steps like these to get them started:

1. After you finish your heart map, go back and look at your entries with fresh eyes.
2. Try to push beyond the details by keeping in mind the questions "So what?" and "Why is this first time significant to my life?" Digging deeper to find a larger meaning will enable you to take your writing beyond a description to become the foundation of an essay, poem, or memoir.
3. On a separate piece of paper, or in your notebook, use your heart map to begin an essay, poem, or memoir about your first time and why it's meaningful to you.

Figure 3.19 Lily fills her First Time heart map with exuberant writing and drawing about the first time she met her nephew.

Mentor Texts

- Ada, Alma Flor. 1995. *My Name Is María Isabel*. New York: Atheneum Books for Young Readers. (2–5)
- Aliki. 1998. *Marianthe's Story: Painted Words and Spoken Memories*. New York: Greenwillow Books. (K–5)
- Applegate, Katherine. 2008. *Home of the Brave*. New York: Square Fish. (5–9)
- Bell, Cece. 2014. *El Deafo*. New York: Harry N. Abrams. (3–7)
- Bunting, Eve. 2006. *One Green Apple*. New York: Clarion Books. (Preschool–3)
- Choi, Yangsook. 2003. *The Name Jar*. New York: Dell Dragonfly Books. (Preschool–2)
- Grimes, Nikki. 2013. *Words with Wings*. Honesdale, PA: WordSong. (3+)
- Gunning, Monica. 2013. *America, My New Home*. Honesdale, PA: WordSong. (2–6)
- Herrera, Juan Felipe. 2013. *The Upside Down Boy: El niño de cabeza*. San Francisco: Children's Book. (K+)
- Hilton, Marilyn. 2015. *Full Cicada Moon*. New York: Dial Books. (3–7)
- Hunt, Lynda Mullaly. 2013. *One for the Murphys*. New York: Puffin Books. (5+)
- LaMarche, Jim. 2002. *The Raft*. New York: HarperCollins. (K–3)
- Lombard, Jenny. 2008. *Drita, My Homegirl*. New York: Puffin Books. (3–7)
- MacLachlan, Patricia. 1994. *All the Places to Love*. New York: HarperCollins. (Preschool–3)
- Recorvits, Helen. 2014. *My Name Is Yoon*. New York: Square Fish. (Preschool–3)
- Spinelli, Jerry. 1998. *Knots in My Yo-Yo String*. New York: Ember. (3–7)

6

Last Time Heart Map

Introduction

I'm not very good at endings. I even hesitate to throw out old papers, clothes, and shoes, and it's very tough to say good-bye to friends and relatives.

I remember the last time I saw my grandfather. He stepped out of the screen door and walked toward our car, packed for our long journey home. As we drove down the dusty driveway, I turned to look behind. My grandfather stood there like a mirage on the dusty road. It was the last time I would ever see him. He died the following spring at ninety-three years old.

A Last Time heart map doesn't have to be about something sad, or even about seeing a person for the last time. It could be about the last time you lived in your country or your city or town, or the last time you visited a special place, or the last time you went to a particular school—or any other important pivot point in your life.

Last times are forks in the road where life shifts, and it's often during these times we discover something important about ourselves.

Try This

Writers can use the Last Time Heart Map Template to record meaningful last times. The image in this heart map template is a nod to endings, with the gradually-fading flourish at the bottom of the heart that resembles the looping end of a signature. As they map their last times, students might discover

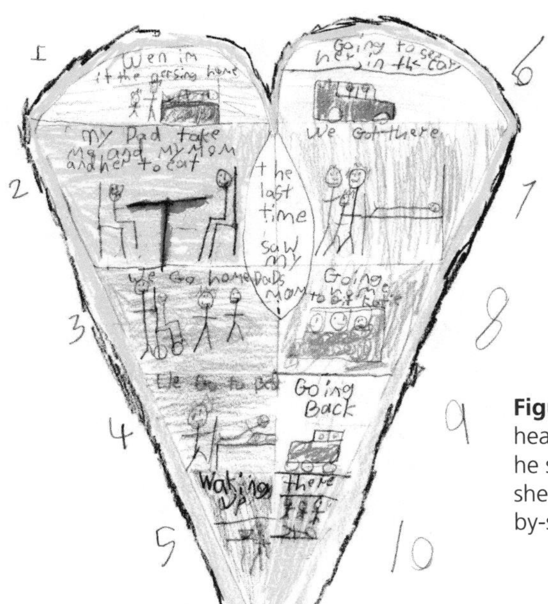

Figure 3.20 Erick's Last Time heart map is about the last time he saw his grandmother before she died. His heart map is a step-by-step account in pictures.

Last Time Heart Map Template

Here are some ideas you might include on your Last Time heart map.

The Last Time You . . .

- saw or spent time in your country or city or town
- saw a grandparent, relative, or friend
- saw a pet
- saw your home where you used to live
- did something that you've never done again
- played a sport or did an activity that you haven't done since
- considered yourself a child, or another aspect of yourself.

Name: ______________________

____

Date: ______________________

that sometimes last times and first times intertwine. For example, they might map the last time they lived in a place they loved—which could also be the beginning of living in a new place they love equally as much; or the last time they saw a person they loved could mean memories that deepen and grow even more cherished over time.

Writing Ideas

This heart map supports writing in personal narrative, essay, poem, and memoir. Ask your students to follow these steps to begin writing:

1. After you finish your heart map, go back and look at it with fresh eyes.
2. Try to push beyond the details by keeping in mind the questions "So what?" and "Why is this last time significant to my life?" Digging deeper to find a larger meaning will enable you to take your writing beyond a description to become the foundation of an essay, poem, or memoir.
3. On a separate piece of paper, or in your notebook, use your heart map to begin an essay, poem, or memoir about your last time and why it's meaningful to you.

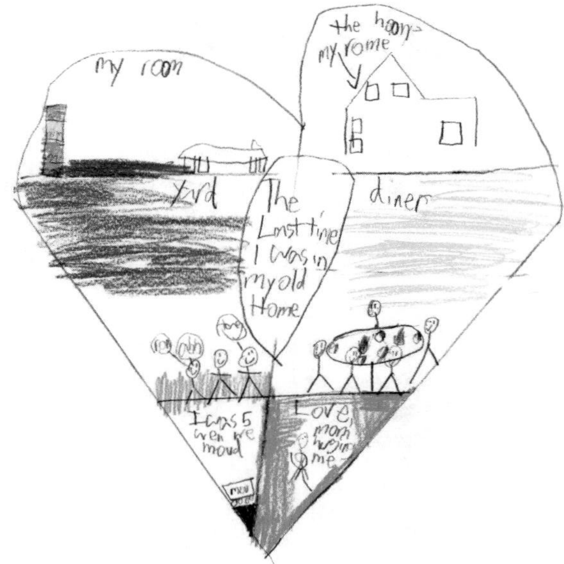

Figure 3.21 Ryan's Last Time heart map is about the last time he was in his old home. When his teacher, Mary Glover, conferred with him about writing from his heart map, he looked at his paper briefly and then asked, "Would it be OK if I made a heart map for home? I think I need one."

Mentor Texts

- Bunting, Eve. 2015. *Yard Sale*. Somerville, MA: Candlewick. (Preschool–2)
- Fletcher, Ralph. 2005. *Marshfield Dreams: When I Was a Kid*. New York: Henry Holt. (5–10)
- MacLachlan, Patricia. 1998. *What You Know First*. New York: HarperCollins. (Preschool–3)
- Mohr, Nicholasa. 1999. *Felita*. New York: Puffin Books. (3–7)
- Pérez, Amada Irma. 2013. *My Diary from Here to There: Mi diario de aquí hasta allá*. San Francisco: Children's Book Press. (K+)

Family Quilt Heart Map

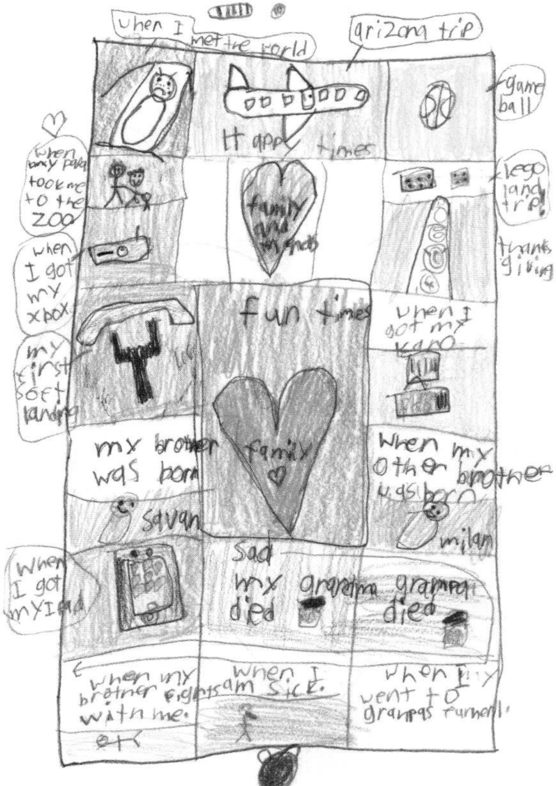

Figure 3.22
Kahnan's Family Quilt heart map

Introduction

My uncle handwrote our family tree on white butcher-block paper and rolled it up in a tight scroll. When I visited him, he unrolled it, and it reached from one side of the living room to the other. Seeing all those names stretched across the room connected me to my larger, extended family, but it also left me wanting more. Beyond my ancestors' names, dates of birth, marriages, and deaths, I wanted to lean over that silent butcher-block paper and listen to their secrets, stories, and dreams.

A family tree is only an outline—a blueprint of a family. When I think of family stories, the tradition of quilt making comes to mind. One of my favorite narratives about keeping family memories alive is *The Keeping Quilt*, by Patricia Polacco (2001). In this story, a quilt is made from scraps of fabric worn by family members across generations; Great-Gramma Anna's babushka and Uncle Vladimir's shirts preserve the memories of home for this Russian family. Family quilts are often passed from one generation to another, and so too are family stories, bound together by gathered scraps of woven memories.

Try This

Writers can map the people, stories, memories, rituals, and traditions on their own Family Quilt heart maps. When creating this map, students can consider some of the ideas and questions on the Family Quilt Heart Map Template.

Figure 3.23
Mallory's Family Quilt heart map

Family Quilt Heart Map Template

Is there a special person or persons in your family whom you would place in the center of your heart map? Describe why they are special.

- What family stories or memories can you include?
- Write down any family songs, traditions, rituals, or foods that make your family unique.
- Write any family stories that your family tells and retells to each other.
- You can also include details of place such as a family home or town, city, or country where your family comes from and how that has shaped your family memories and stories.

Name: ______________________

____

Date: ______________________

Figure 3.24 Sofia's Family Quilt heart map

If writers don't know any family stories, they can interview a parent, a grandparent, an aunt, or an uncle and see what they can learn. They can also look at family photos and write about the details of their facial expressions, their clothes, and the world they see around them.

Writing Ideas

The Family Quilt heart map works best to support small moment writing, personal narrative, memoir, and poetry. Here are some possible entry points for students:

- Choose one entry on your Family Quilt heart map, and in your writer's notebook, or on a separate sheet of paper, brainstorm memories using sensory details (sight, hearing, touch, smell, and taste).
- If you're writing a memoir, ask yourself what the focus of your memoir is and how family helps make you who you are.
- Write a poem describing one of the entries about family on your heart map.
- Read some of the suggested mentor texts about family to see how other authors focused stories on family.

Mentor Texts

- Garza, Carmen Lomas. 2000. *In My Family/En mi familia*. San Francisco: Children's Book Press. (1+)
- ———. 2005. *Family Pictures/Cuadros de familia*. San Francisco: Children's Book Press. (1+)
- Greenfield, Eloise. 1993. *Childtimes: A Three-Generation Memoir*. New York: HarperCollins. (4–6)
- ———. 1996. *Grandpa's Face*. New York: Puffin Books. (Preschool–3)
- Grimes, Nikki. 2007. *Oh, Brother!* New York: Greenwillow Books. (1–5)
- Guback, Georgia. 1994. *Luka's Quilt*. New York: Greenwillow Books. (Preschool–3)
- Hunt, Lynda Mullaly. 2013. *One for the Murphys*. New York: Puffin Books. (5+)
- Laminack, Lester L. 2004. *Saturdays and Teacakes*. Atlanta: Peachtree. (K+)
- MacLachlan, Patricia. 1998. *What You Know First*. New York: HarperCollins. (Preschool–3)

- Manning, Maurie J. 2008. *Kitchen Dance*. New York: Clarion Books. (Preschool–3)
- Mathis, Sharon Bell. 2006. *The Hundred Penny Box*. New York: Puffin Books. (1–4)
- McKissack, Patricia C. 2008. *Stitchin' and Pullin': A Gee's Bend Quilt*. New York: Random House Books for Young Readers. (K–4)
- Polacco, Patricia. 2001. *The Keeping Quilt*. New York: Simon and Schuster/ Paula Wiseman Books. (Preschool–3)
- Steptoe, Javaka, illus. 2013. *In Daddy's Arms I Am Tall: African Americans Celebrating Fathers*. New York: Lee and Low Books. (3–6)
- Wong, Janet. 2008. *The Rainbow Hand: Poems About Mothers and Children*. North Charleston, SC: BookSurge. (4–6)
- Woodson, Jacqueline. 2014. *Brown Girl Dreaming*. New York: Nancy Paulsen Books. (5+)

Poetry

- Blanco, Richard. 1998a. "Mango No. 61." In *City of a Hundred Fires*. Pittsburgh: University of Pittsburgh Press. (High school)
- ———. 1998b. "Mother Picking Produce." In *City of a Hundred Fires*. Pittsburgh: University of Pittsburgh Press. (High school)
- Clifton, Lucille. 1987. "sister." In *The Collected Poems of Lucille Clifton*, Rochester: NY: BOA Editions, Ltd. (6+)
- Espaillat, Rhina P. 1998. "Bilingual/bilingüe." In *Where Horizons Go*. Kirksville, MO: New Odyssey. (High school)
- Gorrell, Nancy. 1997. "Blueberry Pie." In *Reflections on a Gift of Watermelon Pickle . . . and Other Modern Verse*, 2d edition, edited by Stephen Dunning, Edward Lueders, and Hugh Smith. Boston: Addison Wesley. (6+)
- Kennedy, Caroline, ed. 2013. *Poems to Learn by Heart*. New York: Disney-Hyperion. (5+)

8

My Name Heart Map

Introduction

Our names are part of who we are. Some names have been in the family for generations and are memorials to people we don't want to forget, and some names were chosen for other reasons—a parent loves a particular place, like *Aurora* or *Texas*, or a word, like *Velvet*, or a quality he or she wants his or her child to have, like *Hope*.

My name, Georgia, came from my grandfather, George, of Irish roots, who grew up on a tobacco farm called Four Oaks in rural North Carolina.

When I was born, my two-year-old sister had other plans for my name. She couldn't say *Georgia*, so she said *Doty* instead. It stuck. I wore that name, *Doty*, like a borrowed coat throughout childhood until I went to college. At seventeen I stepped out of my nickname and into my real name. A grown-up name. I was ready, like a caterpillar breaking out of its chrysalis, ready to fly.

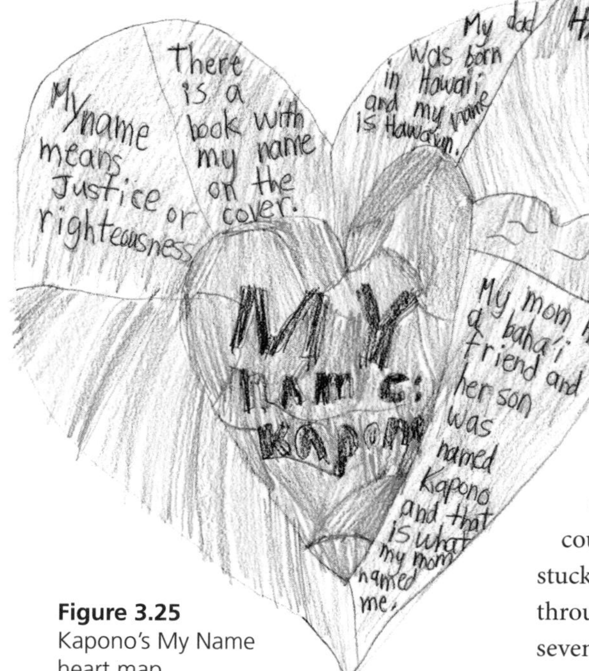

Figure 3.25
Kapono's My Name heart map

Try This

Students can begin to explore their names by using the My Name Heart Map Template. After writing their name in the small heart in the center, writers can explore the stories behind their names to discover how their name has shaped their identity and made them who they are. Writers can explore different aspects of their names by using some of the questions and ideas on the My Name Heart Map Template.

Writing Ideas

This heart map can support writing personal narrative, essay, and poetry. Students might use one of the following prompts to begin writing:

- Is there one entry on your My Name heart map that stands out for you that you could stretch out and write a longer piece about? As you read over your heart map, ask yourself, "Where does my story, essay, or poem begin?" Begin writing a personal narrative or essay about your name.
- Write a poem about one of the entries on your My Name heart map that catches your heart.

My Name Heart Map Template

Place your name in the center of your heart map, in the small heart.

Include details around the heart such as these:

- the story behind your name (if you don't know the story, ask someone who may know why you were named as you were)
- whom you were named after, and why
- how you feel about your name
- what your name means to you
- your nickname and where the nickname came from
- the name teachers use
- the name friends use
- if you've ever been teased about or complimented on your name
- interesting facts or stories about your name
- questions you have about your name.

Name: ______________________

____

Date: ______________________

Figure 3.26 Tavi made a heart map about his real name, Gustavo. He even looked up what his name meant.

Figure 3.27 Kaiden's My Name heart map

- Write an acrostic poem with your name. Write your name vertically down the page with one letter for each line, like this:

  G is for gatherer of words
  E is for ear, listens and loves the sounds
  of poetry
  O is for observer
  R is for finding the perfect rhythm
  G is for a gentle heart
  I is for imagery in her writing
  A is for awe of the world.

Think of verbs, nouns, and adjectives that describe you. Brainstorm a few words. Don't just write the first words that come to mind. Surprise your reader. Look in the thesaurus. Identify traits and qualities about yourself that maybe nobody knows.

Mentor Texts

- Ada, Alma Flor. 1995. *My Name Is María Isabel*. New York: Atheneum Books for Young Readers. (2–5)
- Alexander, Kwame. 2014a. "At First." In *The Crossover*, 8–9. New York: HMH Books for Young Readers. (5–7)
- ———. 2014b. "Filthy McNasty." In *The Crossover*, 10. New York: HMH Books for Young Readers. (5–7)
- ———. 2014c. "How I Got My Nickname." In *The Crossover*, 6–7. New York: HMH Books for Young Readers. (5–7)
- ———. 2014d. "Josh Bell." In *The Crossover*, 4–5. New York: HMH Books for Young Readers. (5–7)
- Choi, Yangsook. 2003. *The Name Jar*. New York: Dell Dragonfly Books. (Preschool–2)
- Cisneros, Sandra. 1991. "My Name." In *The House on Mango Street*. New York: Vintage Books. (7+)
- Henkes, Kevin. 2008. *Chrysanthemum*. New York: Mulberry Books. (Preschool–3)

- Johnston, Tony. 2003. "American Names." In *Any Small Goodness: A Novel of the Barrio*. New York: Scholastic Paperbacks. (4–7)
- Recorvits, Helen. 2014. *My Name Is Yoon*. New York: Square Fish. (Preschool–3)
- Rylant, Cynthia. 2000. *The Old Woman Who Named Things*. New York: HMH Books for Young Readers. (Preschool–3)
- Woodson, Jacqueline. 2014. "A Girl Named Jack." In *Brown Girl Dreaming*. New York: Nancy Paulsen Books. (5+)

Poetry

- Collins, Billy. 2002. "The Names." www.poemhunter.com/poem/the-names-3/. (10+)
- Larios, Julie. 2013. "Names." In *The Poetry Friday Anthology for Middle School: Poems for the School Year with Connections to the Common Core*, edited Sylvia Vardell and Janet Wong, 47. Princeton, NJ: Pomelo Books. (6+)

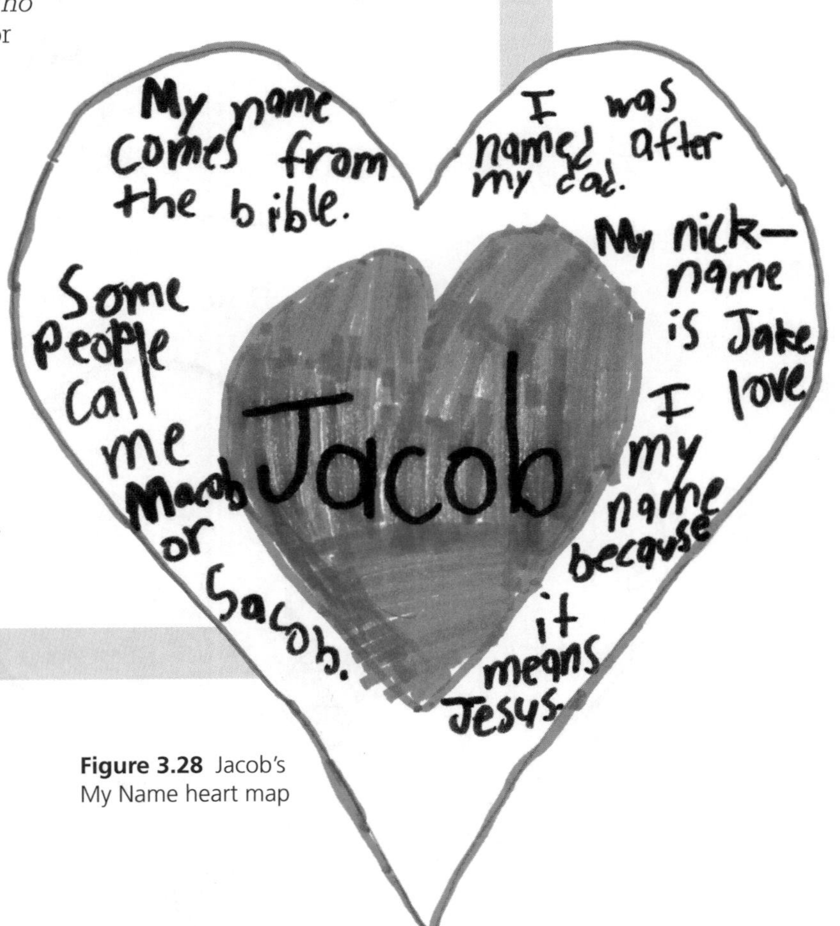

Figure 3.28 Jacob's My Name heart map

9

My Pet or Favorite Animal Heart Map

Introduction

Animals have been the inspiration for stories and poems for centuries because they stay in our hearts like friends and family do.

Figure 3.29 Madison, a second grader in Margaret Simon's class, created a heart map about her cat Pancake.

My dog, Pupster, is ten years old now and feels like an old friend. Here is a short piece I wrote about him when he was a puppy:

> He gallops, ears back, free as the wind like he's Lassie except smaller than a ferret, covered with bristle brown fur, shaggy hair covering his eyes, his tail more like Wilbur the pig than a dog's. Passersby always say, "He's so ugly!" and, "He looks like Yoda or a gremlin!" But everyone agrees on one thing: he's adorable. A rescue dog. Rescued as a pup, and woven into his personality: loyalty, love, and a lick for everyone.

Try This

Students can use the My Pet or Favorite Animal Heart Map Template to map the memories, feelings, and connection they have with either a pet or a favorite animal. This template could be an emotional map of how they feel about a pet or animal to inspire their writing in narrative or a poem, or contain facts and information to guide nonfiction writing.

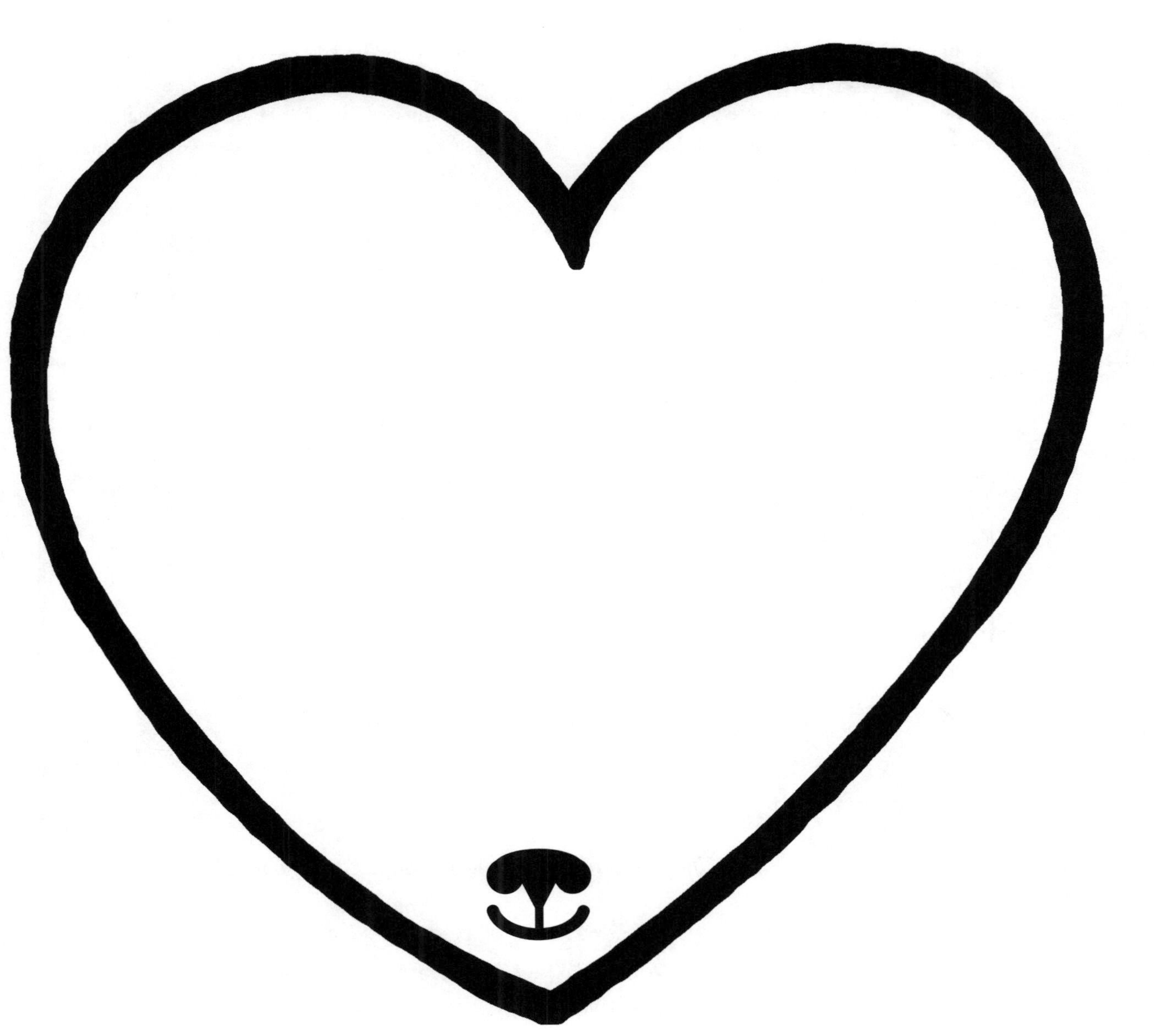

My Pet or Favorite Animal Heart Map Template

Use the My Pet or Favorite Animal Heart Map Template and draw a picture or write the name of your pet or favorite animal in the center of your heart. For a pet heart map, you might include some of the following:

- the story of how you got your pet or when you first saw her
- how you feel about your pet and what he means to you
- a description of what he looks like
- habits or rituals
- adorableness or loveable traits
- favorite foods
- where she likes to sleep
- treasures: favorite toys, places to go, and so on
- what he does during the day
- what she likes to play.

For a favorite animal heart map, you might include some of the following:

- why it's your favorite animal
- where and when you first saw it
- what traits make it your favorite
- a drawing or description of any stories about or a mental picture of your animal
- information or facts about your animal
- questions you have.

Name: ______________________

____

Date: ______________________

heart map
puppy
small puppy
name is puppy
I had him since
I was two
I lose her I
cry
She always sleeps
with me
puppy has cute
and I love
to make clothes
for him
stuffed animal

ears that were
atached to him
but since I had
him so long they
poped off.

Figure 3.30 Sophia didn't have a pet, so she made a heart map about her stuffed animal puppy and then drafted a list poem.

The connection writers feel for their pets or animals is well documented—from Edgar Allen Poe's cat sitting on his shoulder as he wrote poems, to the fifty peacocks that Flannery O'Connor kept in her yard because she thought they were beautiful.

Writing Ideas

This heart map can support writing in small moment writing; personal narrative; personal, opinion, or persuasive essay; poetry; feature article; and informational nonfiction. Ask students to try at least one of these ideas:

- Write a persuasive essay or letter to convince a parent to get you a pet. (See *I Wanna Iguana*, by Karen Orloff [2004], in the list of mentor texts.) State your reasons clearly to be most persuasive.
- Write a poem or story from the point of view of your pet or favorite animal. Imagine what the world would look like—what you would see and hear—if you were your pet or animal. Consider where it lives, how it behaves, what it eats. You might try ending your piece with an interesting fact about your pet or animal.
- Write a biography of your pet or animal (author Virginia Woolf wrote a biography of the writer Elizabeth Barrett Browning's cocker spaniel called *Flush: A Biography* [1997]). Read your heart map to see which are the best details to include in your biography.
- Write an informational piece about your pet or animal. Brainstorm what you know. What questions do you have? Think about the focus of your piece. Will you want to do some more reading or research to add to what you already know? Does your pet or animal have any interesting or unusual traits? Use that as a starting point for your writing.

Mentor Texts

- Appelt, Kathi. 2010. *The Underneath*. New York: Atheneum Books for Young Readers. (5–9)
- Creech, Sharon. 2001. *Love That Dog: A Novel*. New York: HarperCollins. (3–7)
- ———. 2010. *Hate That Cat: A Novel*. New York: HarperCollins. (3–7)
- DiCamillo, Kate. 2015. *Because of Winn-Dixie*. Cambridge, MA: Candlewick. (4–7)

- Engle, Margarita. 2014. *Mountain Dog*. New York: Square Fish. (3–7)
- George, Kristine O'Connell. 2002. *Little Dog and Duncan*. New York: Clarion Books. (Preschool–3)
- Heard, Georgia. 1997. *Creatures of Earth, Sea, and Sky*. Honesdale, PA: WordSong. (1–4)
- Hobbs, Valerie. 2009. *Sheep*. New York: Square Fish. (3–7)
- Kalman, Maira. 2003. *What Pete Ate from A–Z*. New York: Puffin Books. (Preschool–2)
- ———. 2015. *Beloved Dog*. New York: Penguin. (3+)
- Leedy, Loreen. 2003. *Mapping Penny's World*. New York: Square Fish. (K–3)
- Lewis, J. Patrick, ed. 2012. *National Geographic Book of Animal Poetry: 200 Poems with Photographs That Squeak, Soar, and Roar!* Washington, DC: National Geographic Children's Books. (Preschool–3)
- Oliver, Mary. 2015. *Dog Songs: Poems*. New York: Penguin Books. (High school+)
- Orloff, Karen Kaufman. 2004. *I Wanna Iguana*. New York: G. P. Putnam's Sons Books for Young Readers. (Preschool–3)
- Paschkis, Julie. 2015. *Flutter and Hum: Animal Poems/Aleteo y zumbido: poemas de animals*. New York: Henry Holt. (K–4)
- Pennypacker, Sara. 2016. *Pax*. New York: Balzer and Bray. (4–7)
- Rylant, Cynthia. 1988. *Every Living Thing*. Columbus, OH: Modern Curriculum. (4+)
- ———. 2000. *The Old Woman Who Named Things*. New York: HMH Books for Young Readers. (Preschool–3)
- Thorne, Pete. 2015. *Old Faithful: Dogs of a Certain Age*. New York: Harper Design. (High school)
- Wardlaw, Lee. 2015. *Won Ton and Chopstick: A Cat and Dog Tale Told in Haiku*. New York: Henry Holt. (Preschool–3)

10

Gratitude Heart Map

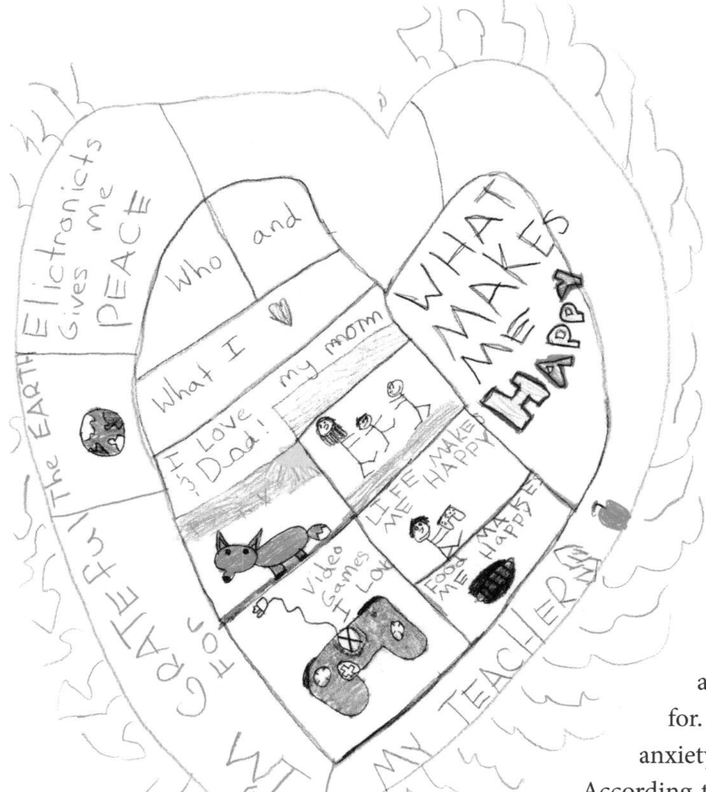

Figure 3.31 William's Gratitude heart map

Introduction

Every night when I was a girl, I closed my eyes and said my prayers before I went to sleep. My mother sat patiently beside me, listening as I slowly and sleepily named everything I was grateful for. I didn't know it at the time but I was doing what Maya Angelou advised: "Let gratitude be the pillow upon which you kneel to say your nightly prayer."

We all have things, people, and experiences that we're thankful for. When we focus on them, worry, anxiety, and sadness can be eased. According to an article by Alex Korb (2012), two researchers discovered that young adults who kept "gratitude journals" showed a greater increase in determination, attention, and enthusiasm.

When we write, we celebrate the beautiful, the awe-inspiring, and the simple joys in our lives. The act of paying conscious attention to what we're thankful for—the big things and the small—can help us not only gather writing ideas but also slow down and notice the bounty we're surrounded by.

Alice Walker (1983) writes about her gratitude for being able to see beauty in the world as she describes seeing the desert for the first time.

> I remember:
>
> I am in the desert for the first time. I fall totally in love with it. I am so overwhelmed by its beauty, I confront for the first time, consciously, the meaning of the doctor's words years ago: "Eyes are sympathetic. If one is blind, the other will likely become blind too." I realize I have dashed about the world madly, looking at this, looking at that, storing up images against the fading of the light. But I might have missed seeing the desert! The shock of that possibility—and gratitude for over twenty-five years of sight—sends me literally to my knees. Poem after poem comes—which is perhaps how poets pray.

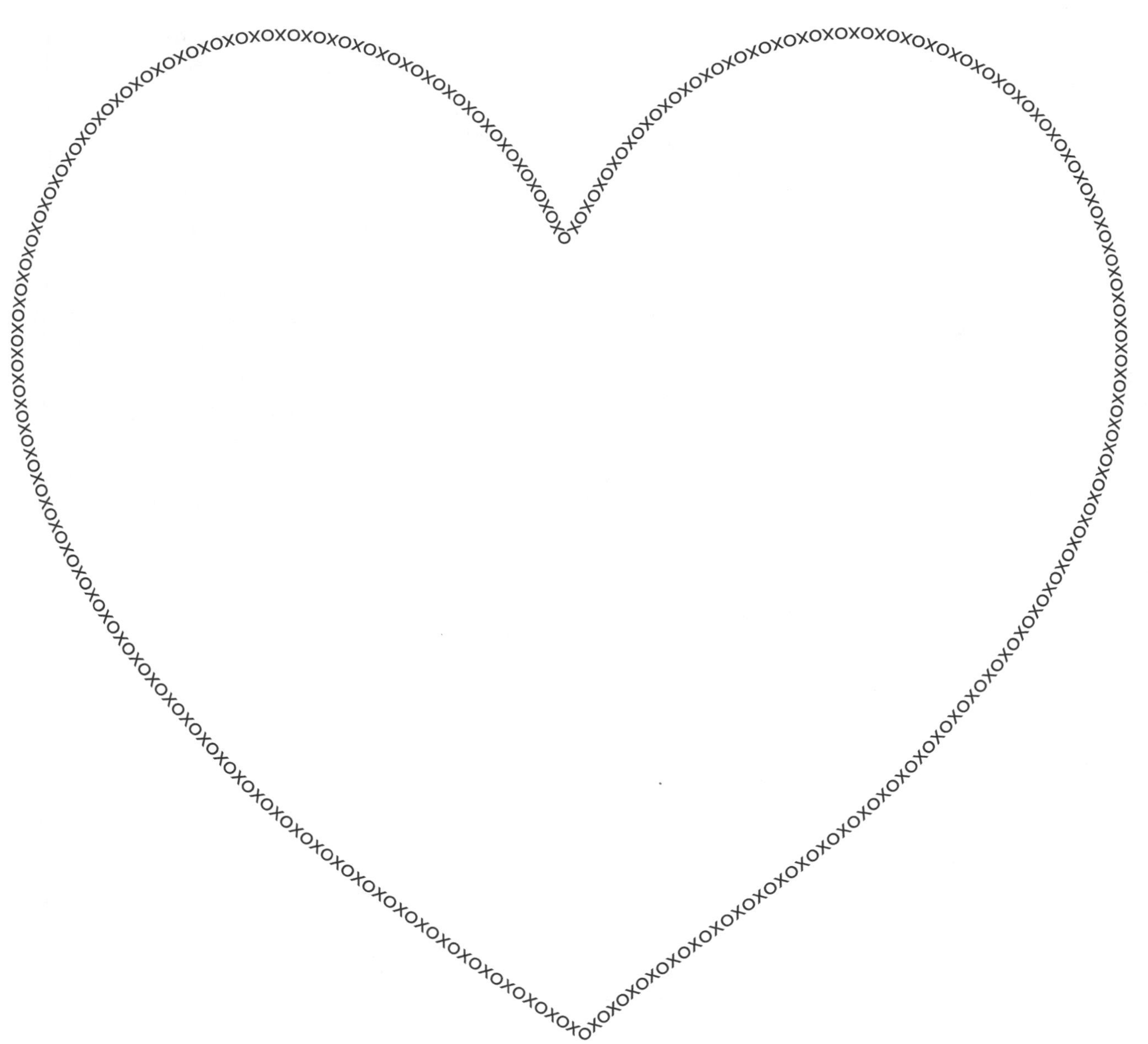

Gratitude Heart Map Template

Create a Gratitude heart map by mapping the following:

- people you're grateful for
- what makes you happy
- what brings you peace of mind or comfort
- whom or what you love
- things that inspire you
- things you love and observe in the world
- places you love
- events or experiences that were unexpected or surprising.

Don't add only huge things, but also things that are easy to take for granted in everyday life:

- family
- a place to sleep
- food
- friends.

Name: ______________________

____

Date: ______________________

Try This

Writers can explore what they are grateful for with the Gratitude Heart Map Template. A heart framed by *x*'s and *o*'s—"hugs" and "kisses"—in this case symbolizes what in the world writers are grateful for: big abstract things, and also tiny particulars. See the template for a few tips you can offer your students as they use heart mapping to explore the idea of gratitude.

Writing Ideas

The Gratitude heart map can support writing personal essay, memoir, letter, apostrophe poem, and blog or writer's notebook entries. Students can respond to one of the following to generate writing:

- Create a list poem from all the entries on your Gratitude heart map, and then write an ending that surprises or has a twist to it.
- Choose one idea as the seed for a personal essay; build your essay around this idea, and explain why you're grateful.
- Write a letter or letter poem (apostrophe poem) addressing someone whom you are thankful for and giving the reasons why.
- Organize your memoir around what you're grateful for.
- Go for a gratitude walk—bring your notebook with your heart map in it and write down all that you see that you're grateful for.
- Start a daily gratitude blog or journal beginning with what you've put on your heart map.

Mentor Texts

- Bucchino, John. 2003. *Grateful: A Song of Giving Thanks*. New York: HarperCollins. (Preschool–4)
- de la Peña, Matt. 2015. *Last Stop on Market Street*. New York: G. P. Putnam's Sons Books for Young Readers. (Preschool–K)
- dePaola, Tomie. 2015. *Look and Be Grateful*. New York: Holiday House. (Preschool+)
- Grimes, Nikki. 2006. *Thanks a Million*. New York: Greenwillow Books. (1–5)
- Lawson, JonArno. 2015. *Sidewalk Flowers*. Toronto: Groundwood Books. (Preschool–2)

- Parr, Todd. 2012. *The Thankful Book*. New York: Little, Brown Books for Young Readers. (Preschool–1)
- Polacco, Patricia. 2012. *Thank You, Mr. Falker*. New York: Philomel Books. (K–3)
- Spinelli, Eileen. 2015. *Thankful*. Grand Rapids, MI: Zonderkidz. (Preschool–3)
- Walker, Alice. 1983. "Beauty: When the Other Dancer Is the Self." In *In Search of Our Mothers' Gardens: Womanist Prose*. San Diego: Harcourt Brace Jovanovich.
- Willems, Mo. 2016. *The Thank You Book*. New York: Disney-Hyperion. (1–3)
- Wood, Douglas. 2005. *Secret of Saying Thanks*. New York: Simon & Schuster Books for Young Readers. (Preschool–3)
- Wyeth, Sharon Dennis. 2002. *Something Beautiful*. New York: Dragonfly Books. (Preschool–2)

Poetry

- Coatsworth, Elizabeth. 1934. "Swift Things Are Beautiful." In *Away Goes Sally*, 60. Bathgate, ND: Bethlehem Books. (3+)
- Hayden, Robert. 2013. "Those Winter Sundays." In *Collected Poems*, edited by Frederick Glaysher. New York: Liveright. (6+)
- Porter, Anne. 2006. "A List of Praises." In *Living Things: Collected Poems*. Hanover, NH: Zoland Books. (6+)
- Strand, Mark. 1980. "From a Litany." In *Selected Poems*. New York: Atheneum. (High school)

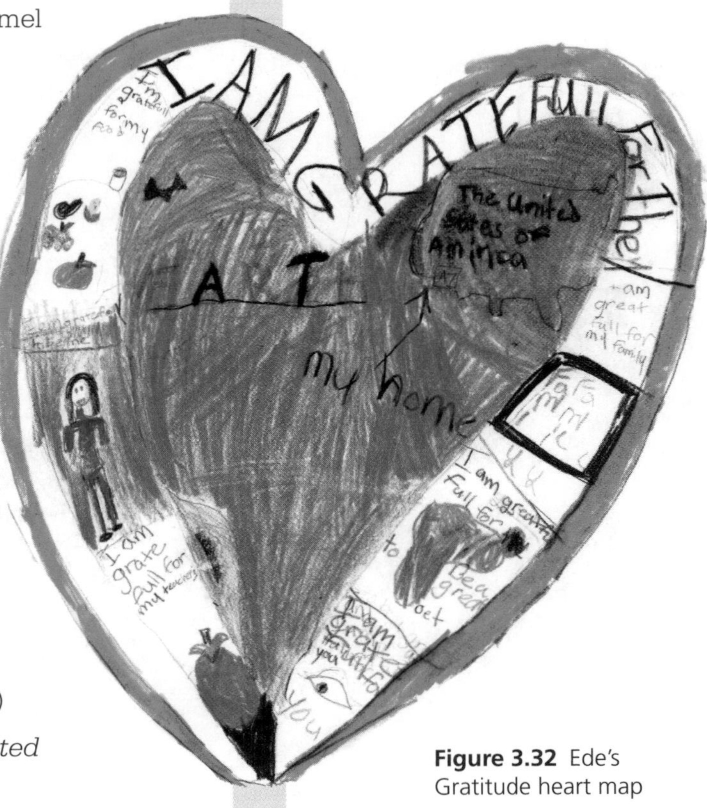

Figure 3.32 Ede's Gratitude heart map

11

Home Is Where My Heart Is Heart Map

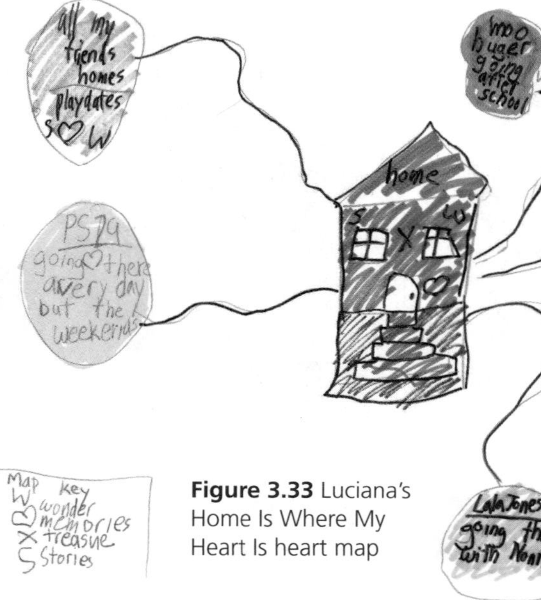

Figure 3.33 Luciana's Home Is Where My Heart Is heart map

Introduction

When I was a girl, my friends and I gathered by the creek next to my house and played kickball, capture the flag, and spud until day turned to dusk and the fireflies twinkled in the darkening trees. On the heart map of my neighborhood, I include the field where we played capture the flag; the sidewalk where we drew hopscotch squares with pink chalk; and my yard in winter, where we rolled and stacked large, round snowballs for snowmen. Above my desk is a wooden plaque that reads Home Is Where the Story Begins. I've written several poems and stories inspired by home, such as the following poem, which was included in the *Poetry Friday Anthology* (2012):

The Winner

Evenings,
we play ball
next to the creek
in our neighbor's field.

I
can't
even
catch
my
breath.

When blue dusk turns to black,
cold grass aches our feet,
trees creep close—
game's over.
Night wins!

Much later, when my home was in new York City, the view out my window inspired many poems and stories.

Try This

The idea of making a map of your home to gather stories and poems came from my friend and colleague Ralph Fletcher in his book *How to Write Your Life Story* (2007).

You can use the Home Is Where My Heart Is Heart Map Template to create a heart map of a home, neighborhood, town, city, or country that holds stories and memories. Start by physically mapping and labeling your home. Draw a map of the houses, apartments, streets, sidewalks, stores, stoplights, parks, basketball courts, or other landmark places that make your home yours.

Then take a memory tour of your map and add memories and stories. You can also take an emotional tour, where you write the feelings underlying your memories.

I've added a key in the margin of the heart map to help writers mark meaningful places that are doorways into writing. Use different-colored pens to mark various locations.

Writing Ideas

This heart map can support writing personal narrative, memoir, essay, and poetry. Give students one of the following activities:

- Write a poem about one place on your heart map. Make a mental movie and write true, exact details from the movie in your mind.
- Think about if each one of your entries could be a chapter in your memoir.
- Read all the entries on your heart map and think about what the connections are between entries. Write about those connections.
- Zoom in on one entry on your heart map and, in a personal narrative or essay, zoom in on one of the most important parts of the story.

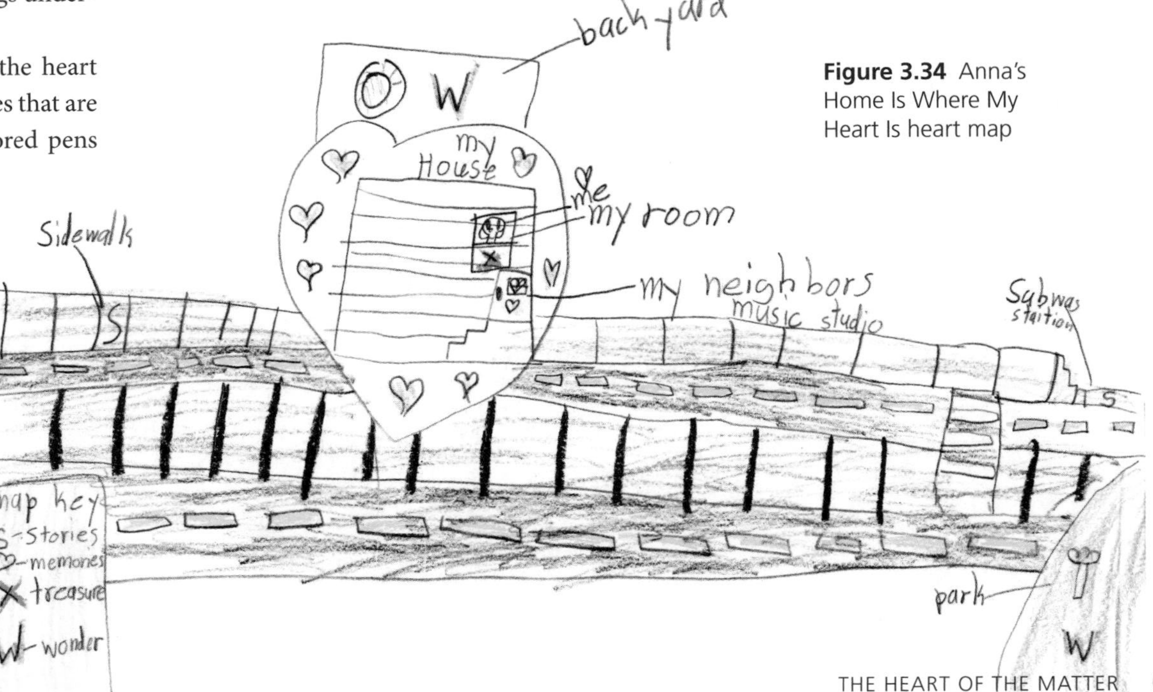

Figure 3.34 Anna's Home Is Where My Heart Is heart map

Home Is Where My Heart Is Heart Map Template

Here are some ideas you might want to include in a Home Is Where My Heart Is heart map:

- a place that's special or memorable to you because it holds important memories
- a place where you gather with your friends to play or explore
- a route to school, to a friend's house, or to another place you frequently visit
- a place where family lives
- the place where you get on the subway or bus
- a place where you walk your dog
- a place where you first did something like ride your bike or play basketball
- the place where your best friend lives
- the stores you visit
- unique and interesting landmarks
- inspiring places in nature.

Name: ______________________

____

Date: ______________________

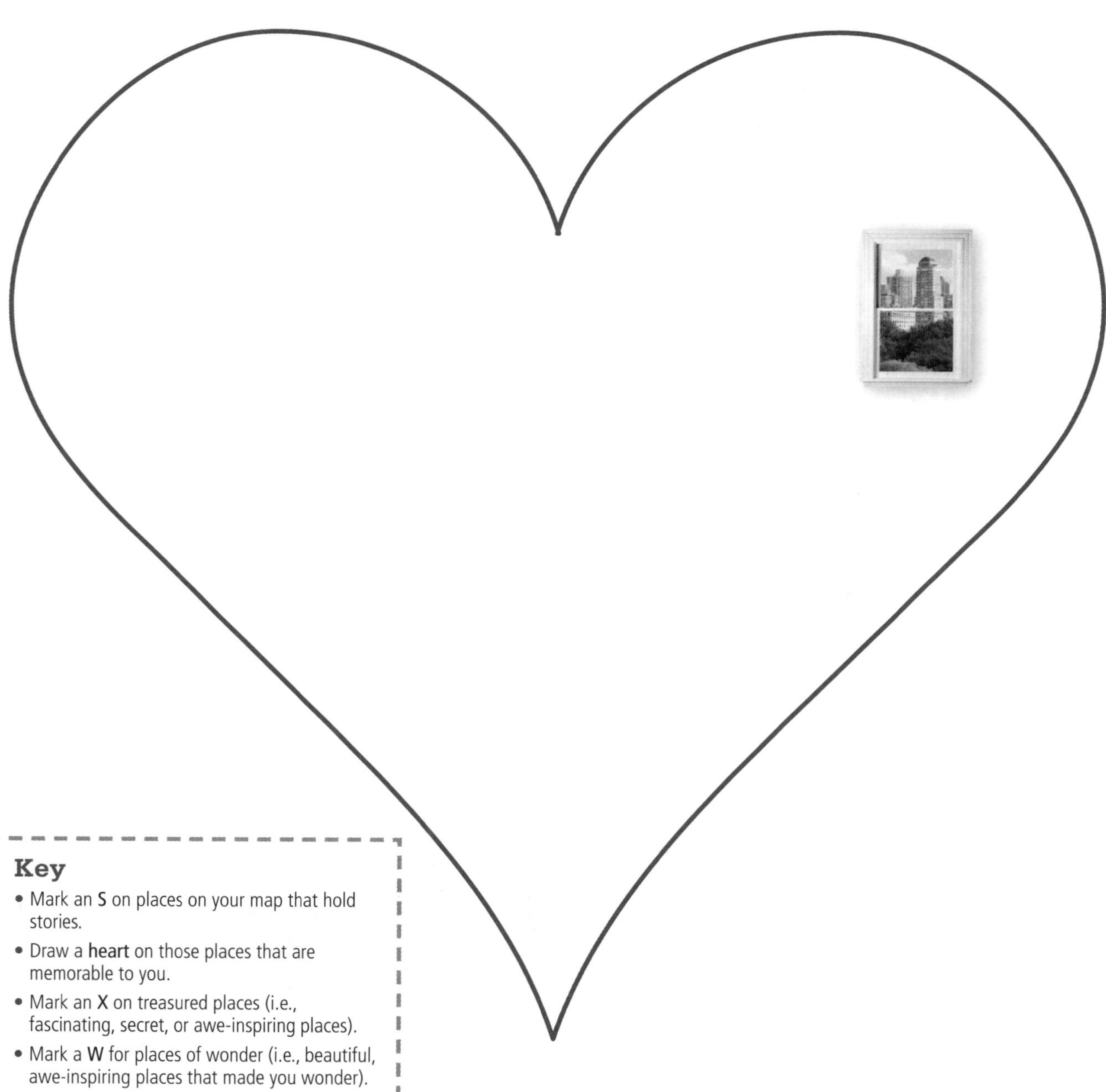

Key

- Mark an **S** on places on your map that hold stories.
- Draw a **heart** on those places that are memorable to you.
- Mark an **X** on treasured places (i.e., fascinating, secret, or awe-inspiring places).
- Mark a **W** for places of wonder (i.e., beautiful, awe-inspiring places that made you wonder).

Mentor Texts

- Bunting, Eve. 2000. *The Memory String*. New York: Clarion Books. (Preschool–3)
- dePaola, Tomie. 2002. *26 Fairmont Avenue*. New York: Puffin Books. (2–5)
- Dowell, Frances O'Roark. 2003. *Where I'd Like to Be*. New York: Atheneum Books for Young Readers. (5–9)
- Fletcher, Ralph. 2005. *Marshfield Dreams: When I Was a Kid*. New York: Henry Holt. (3–5)
- Pérez, Amada Irma. 2013. *My Diary from Here to There: Mi diario de aquí hast allá*. San Francisco: Children's Book Press. (K+)
- Soto, Gary. 2005. *Neighborhood Odes*. Orlando: HMH Books for Young Readers. (2–5)
- Sweeney, Joan. 1998. *Me on the Map*. New York: Dragonfly Books. (Preschool–2)
- Woodson, Jacqueline. 2014. "home again to hall street." In *Brown Girl Dreaming*, 174. New York: Nancy Paulsen Books. (5+)

See also the visual texts on James Mollison's website, http://jamesmollison.com/books/, specifically *Playground* and *Where Children Sleep*. (4+)

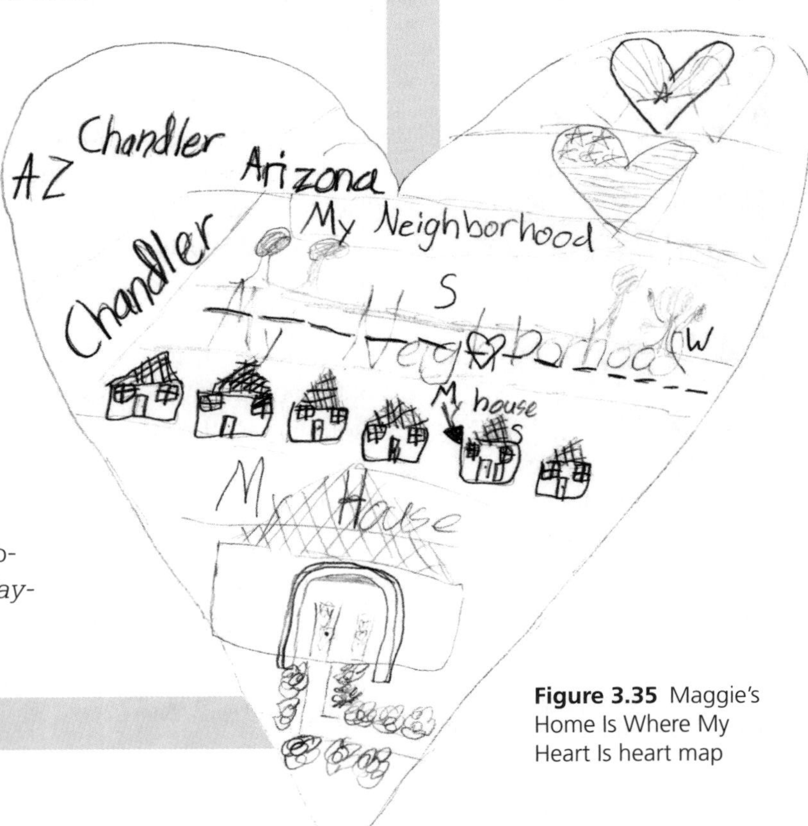

Figure 3.35 Maggie's Home Is Where My Heart Is heart map

12

My Wishes Heart Map

Introduction

Storytellers, writers, and poets have told tales and written poems about wishes for centuries. Wishes have the power to change our lives and the lives of others—and even the world—especially if they're accompanied by action. We wish on stars; birthday candles; coins thrown into wishing wells. We make wishes to summon happiness, love, and peace. Our wishes come from our innermost thoughts and feelings and allow us to imagine possibilities beyond our everyday world.

When I was a girl, I searched the sky for the first star at dusk. When I spotted it, blinking in the darkening sky, I closed my eyes and whispered the little poem my mother taught me (*Star light, star bright, . . .*) and made a wish:

> *I wish that my father will return safely home from the Vietnam War.*
>
> *I wish that all wars will end.*
>
> *I wish that my pet turtle that ran away into the grass will come home.*

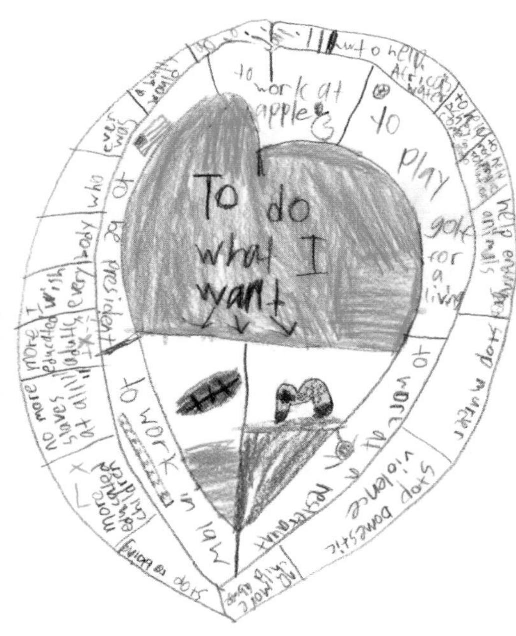

Figure 3.36 Justin wrote his personal wish, *To do what I want*, with specifics of what that means for him, such as *to be president* and *to work in law*, in the center of his heart and wrote his wishes for the world, such as *more educated children*, *more educated adults*, and *no more slaves at all*, around the outer rim of his heart.

Try This

Writers can make wishes by writing them inside the hand-drawn stars on the My Wishes Heart Map Template. Invite students to explore what their personal wishes and wants are, and also what their wishes are for other people and for the world. When I was a girl and made a wish on a star, I knew in my heart what my wish was before I even closed my eyes. Ask students to consider their wishes carefully—not just the wish itself, but also the *why* behind it.

Writing Ideas

The My Wishes heart map can support writing personal narrative, memoir, essay, feature article, opinion essay, and poetry. Ask your students to try one of these activities:

- Write a list poem by gathering all your wishes from your My Wishes heart map. Crack open any words or sentences by adding details. Add an ending with a twist or a surprise.
- Write a memoir where each chapter is a wish you have for your life or the world.

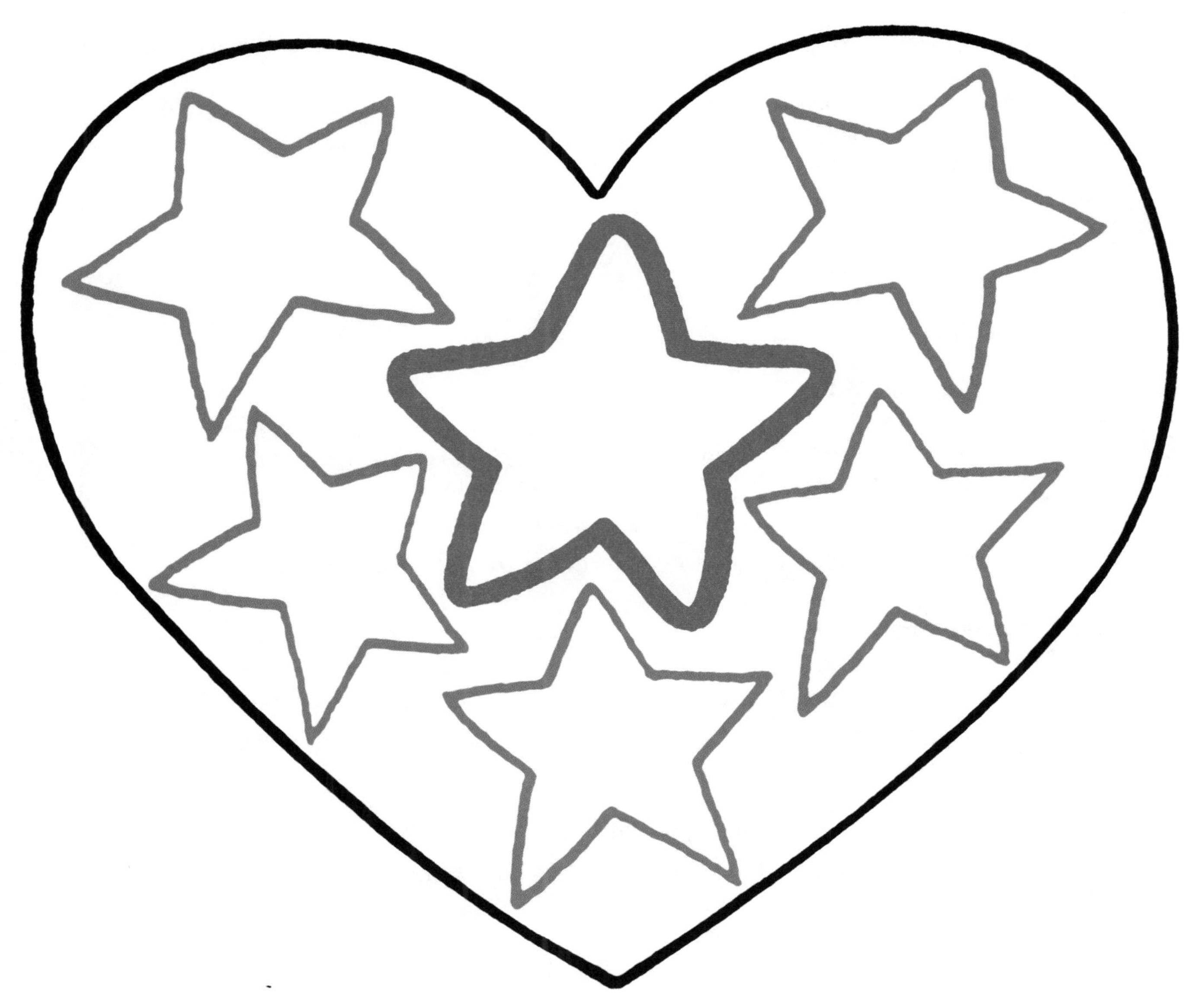

My Wishes Heart Map Template

Write your wishes in the stars on the My Wishes Heart Map Template. You may want to write your main wish in the center of your heart map and then add other wishes around it. You might include any of these:

- personal wishes: wishes about yourself and your life
- wishes for and about other people
- world wishes: positive changes you would like to see in the world.

Name: ______________________

____

Date: ______________________

- Read your wishes and look for connections between them. Think about writing an essay focused on how your wishes fit together.
- Write a feature article about a wish you wrote for the world. Do a little research into your wish to include in your article.
- Write an opinion piece about a world wish on your heart map and explain why and what you truly believe.
- Write a modern-day fairy tale using wishing as the theme.

Mentor Texts

- Ciardi, John. 2015. *The Wish-Tree*. Mineola, NY: Dover. (3–6)
- Dotlich, Rebecca Kai. 2007. "Sky Wish." In *Climb Inside a Poem: Reading and Writing Poetry in the Primary Grades*, by Georgia Heard and Lester Laminack, 10. Portsmouth, NH: FirstHand/Heinemann. (K–2)
- ———. 2016. *The Knowing Book*. Honesdale, PA: Boyds Mills. (K+)
- Gurth, Per-Henrik. 2009. *When Wishes Come True*. Montreal: Lobster. (Preschool–1)
- Jones, Andrea Koehle. 2008. *The Wish Trees*. Bloomington, IN: Author House. (Preschool–2)
- Perkins, Lynne Rae. 2005. *Criss Cross*. New York: Greenwillow Books. (6–9)
- Rosenthal, Amy Krouse. 2015. *I Wish You More*. San Francisco: Chronicle Books. (K–3)
- Sidman, Joyce. 2013. *What the Heart Knows: Chants, Charms and Blessings*. Boston: HMH Books for Young Readers. (7+)
- Stevenson, James. 1995. *I Had a Lot of Wishes*. New York: Greenwillow Books. (2–4)
- Woodson, Jacqueline. 2014. "every wish, one dream." In *Brown Girl Dreaming*, 313. New York: Nancy Paulsen Books. (5+)
- ———. 2014. "wishes." In *Brown Girl Dreaming*, 174. New York: Nancy Paulsen Books. (5+)

You can also share some fairy tales, such as *The Magic Porridge Pot* and *The Fisherman's Wife*, that include making a wish and the dangers of being careless or greedy with wishing for too much.

To inspire students, try making a class wish tree, as conceived by Yoko Ono. Ono, artist and widow of John Lennon, one of the Beatles, has instructions on her website for creating your own wish tree and later sending those wishes to Iceland (see "Wish Trees" at http://imaginepeacetower.com/yoko-onos-wish-trees/). Over a million wishes from people all over the world are permanently stored in the Imagine Peace Tower installation in Iceland, an outdoor work of art in memory of Lennon.

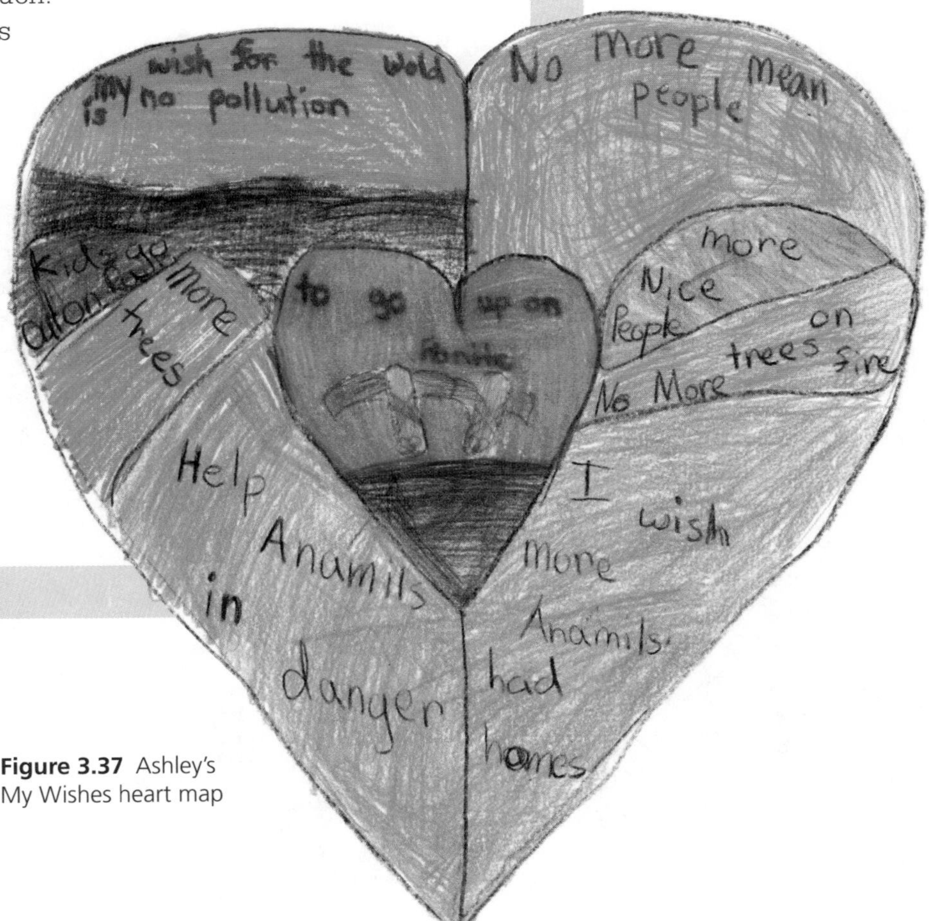

Figure 3.37 Ashley's My Wishes heart map

13

Special Place Heart Map

Introduction

If you closed your eyes and listened to how I described my special places to you, I hope you'd be able to smell the fishy Virginia creek next to my childhood house, or hear the loons echoing across Kusumpee Pond near my family's home in New Hampshire, or see the golden-rowed cornfields on Scuttle Hole Lane as the sun set on Long Island. We become who we are in some ways because of the details of our landscape, the places we come to know growing up. Writers' words are infused with the particulars of place.

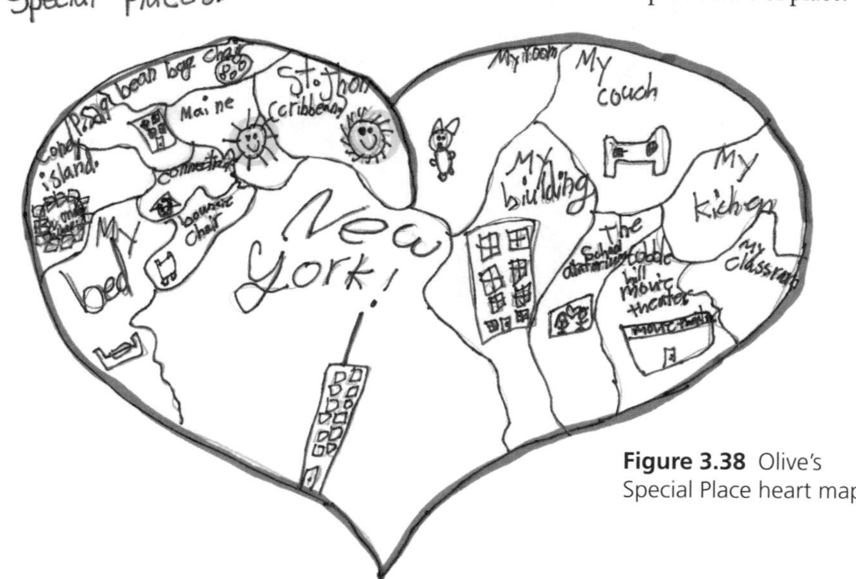

Figure 3.38 Olive's Special Place heart map

Try This

On the Special Place Heart Map Template, invite writers to map the special places in their lives that they know and love intimately. The places we know shape us, and their details stay in our memories. As writers map their special places, encourage them to write their close observations and small specifics to tap into later as they write.

Writing Ideas

The Special Place heart map can support writing personal narrative, memoir, essay, feature article, opinion essay, and poetry. Ask your students to respond to one of these ideas:

- After you select a special place from your heart map, continue to make a mental movie in your mind using all your senses to write a personal narrative, memoir, or essay about your special place.
- Write a poem about a special place on your heart map, focusing on the senses (sight, smell, taste, touch, and sound) or highlighting just one sense through the whole poem.

Special Place Heart Map Template

Begin by mapping several special places, or start with memories of one place. Here are some ideas to include on the heart map:

- a special place you like to explore or play in near your home
- a place where you lived when you were younger
- a special vacation spot
- a place where your grandparents or other relatives live
- a place you've seen that is beautiful and awe-inspiring
- a quiet place where you go to be by yourself to think.

To guide your writing, try the following:

- Ask yourself, "Why is this place special to me?"
- Ask, "What memories do I have of this place?"
- Close your eyes and make a mental movie of your place. Write and/or draw what you see, smell, touch, taste, and hear.

Name: ______________________

____

Date: ______________________

Figure 3.39 Eva's Special Place heart map

- Write a feature article about your special place, researching its history and including information or facts about this place in your article. If appropriate, interview people who live in or know about your place and include their voices by quoting them in the article.
- Write an opinion essay about why your place is special to you and why you think other people would also love it.

Mentor Texts

- Cameron, Ann. 1993. *The Most Beautiful Place in the World*. New York: Yearling. (3–7)
- Giovanni, Nikki. 1997. "Knoxville, Tennessee." In *Reflections on a Gift of a Watermelon Pickle . . . and Other Modern Verse*, 2d edition, edited by Stephen Dunning, Edward Lueders, and Hugh Smith. Boston: Addison Wesley.
- Hopkins, Lee Bennett. 2015. *Amazing Places*. New York: Lee and Low Books. (3–5)
- Kalman, Maira. 1999. *Next Stop, Grand Central*. New York: G. P. Putnam's Sons Books for Young Readers. (Preschool–3)
- MacLachlan, Patricia. 1994. *All the Places to Love*. New York: HarperCollins. (Preschool–3)
- Ringgold, Faith. 1996. *Tar Beach*. New York: Dragonfly Books. (K–3)
- Rothman, Julia. 2014. *Hello NY: An Illustrated Love Letter to the Five Boroughs*. San Francisco: Chronicle Books. (High school)
- Rylant, Cynthia. 1998. *Appalachia: The Voices of Sleeping Birds*. San Diego: Voyager Books. (Preschool–3)

14

Be the Change That You Wish to See in the World Heart Map

Introduction

The great Indian leader Mahatma Gandhi purportedly said these wise words: *Be the change that you wish to see in the world.* His words are a call for us to take action about something we observe in the world that we want to change. Change often starts small—with an observation, a hope that then leads to action.

As a young girl, Malala Yousafzai, the youngest person to receive the Nobel Peace Prize, felt that it was unfair that girls weren't allowed to go to school in Taliban-controlled Pakistan. She started writing a blog expressing her opinion about the Taliban's threat to take away girls' education and then continued to speak out for what she believed despite the danger to her life. No matter how small or big, our actions can change the world.

Try This

Ask students to use the Be the Change That You Wish to See in the World Heart Map Template to think about what they see in the world that they'd like to change and what actions they might take to start making those changes. They can start by asking themselves, "What do I notice in the world that I would like to change? Are there examples of injustice, inequality, or prejudice in my school, neighborhood, town, or city?"

Writers might also use two Be The Change That You Wish to See in the World Heart Map Templates—one to map their concerns about the world, and a second one to map possible solutions or things they can do to help resolve a concern.

Writing Ideas

This heart map supports writing in opinion, persuasive essay, blog entry, letter to the editor, and poetry. Have students choose one entry from their heart map that they feel the strongest about and respond to one of these prompts:

- Write an opinion piece for the school or local newspaper expressing your opinion about something on your heart map.

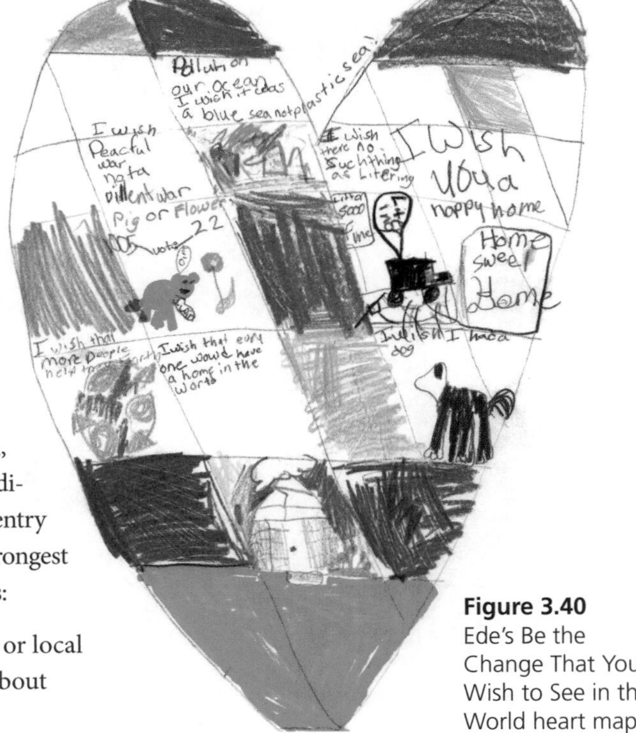

Figure 3.40
Ede's Be the Change That You Wish to See in the World heart map

Be the Change That You Wish to See in the World Heart Map Template

Explore some of the following on your Be the Change That You Wish to See in the World Heart Map Template:

- your concerns about the world
- observations about what you notice in the world that you're concerned about
- what you wish to change in the world
- what action you can take to make the world a better place.

Name: ____________________

____

Date: ____________________

- Write a persuasive essay trying to convince readers about something that concerns you.
- Plan a project. Write it out. Start a blog to voice your concerns like Malala did.
- Write a letter stating how you feel to a newspaper, or the principal of your school if it's a school-related issue, or to the president of the United States.
- Write a poem or a song about the concern you chose.

Figure 3.41 Jonah's Be the Change That You Wish to See in the World heart map

Mentor Texts

- Abouraya, Karen Leggett. 2014. *Malala Yousafzai: Warrior with Words*. Great Neck, NY: StarWalk Kids Media. (Preschool–2)
- Alifirenka, Caitlin, and Martin Ganda. 2015. *I Will Always Write Back: How One Letter Changed Two Lives*. With Liz Welch. New York: Little, Brown Books for Young Readers. (7+)
- Boelts, Maribeth. 2009. *Those Shoes*. Somerville, MA: Candlewick. (K–3)
- Brencher, Hannah. 2015. *If You Find This Letter: My Journey to Find Purpose Through Hundreds of Letters to Strangers: A Memoir*. New York: Howard Books. (10+)
- Bunting, Eve. 1993. *Fly Away Home*. New York: HMH Books for Young Readers. (Preschool–3)
- Chin-Lee, Cynthia. 2005. *Amelia to Zora: Twenty-Six Women Who Changed the World*. Watertown, MA: Charlesbridge. (3–7)
- ———. 2008. *Akira to Zoltan: Twenty-Six Men Who Changed the World*. Watertown, MA: Charlesbridge. (3–7)
- Frank, John. 2014. *Lend a Hand: Poems About Giving*. New York: Lee and Low Books. (Preschool–3)
- Grandin, Temple. 2006. "Seeing in Beautiful, Precise Pictures." *This I Believe* (blog). http://thisibelieve.org/essay/18/. (7+)
- Hallinan, P. K. 2002. *Heartprints*. Nashville: CandyCane. (Preschool–3)

Figure 3.42 Sofia's Be the Change That You Wish to See in the World heart map

Figure 3.43 Mallory's Be the Change That You Wish to See in the World heart map

- Isabella, Jude. 2015. *The Red Bicycle: The Extraordinary Story of One Ordinary Bicycle*. Toronto: Kids Can Press. (3–7)
- Kamkwamba, William. 2016. *The Boy Who Harnessed the Wind*. New York: Puffin Books. (5+)
- Nye, Naomi Shihab. 2008. "Gate A-4." In *Honeybee*, 162–164. New York: Greenwillow Books. (5+)
- Paul, Miranda. 2015. *One Plastic Bag: Isatou Ceesay and the Recycling Women of the Gambia*. Minneapolis: Millbrook. (1–4)
- Winter, Jeanette. 2005. *The Librarian of Basra: A True Story from Iraq*. San Diego: HMH Books for Young Readers. (K–3)
- Woodson, Jacqueline. 2012. *Each Kindness*. New York: Nancy Paulsen Books. (K–3)
- Wyeth, Sharon Dennis. 2002. *Something Beautiful*. New York: Dragonfly Books. (Preschool–2)
- Yousafzai, Malala. 2014. *I Am Malala: How One Girl Stood Up for Education and Changed the World*. Young Readers Edition. With Patricia McCormick. New York: Little Brown Books for Young Readers. (5+)

Students in middle and high school may also appreciate the lyrics in will.i.am's "Yes We Can" in the 2008 song by the Black Eyed Peas (produced by will.i.am) using lyrics from then-Senator (now President) Barack Obama's concession speech in the New Hampshire presidential primary.

Also the lyrics in "A Dream," a 2006 song by Common on the *Freedom Writers* soundtrack (Hollywood Records), which quotes excerpts from Martin Luther King Jr.'s "I Have a Dream" speech.

The CitizenKid series from Kids Can Press is another great resource.

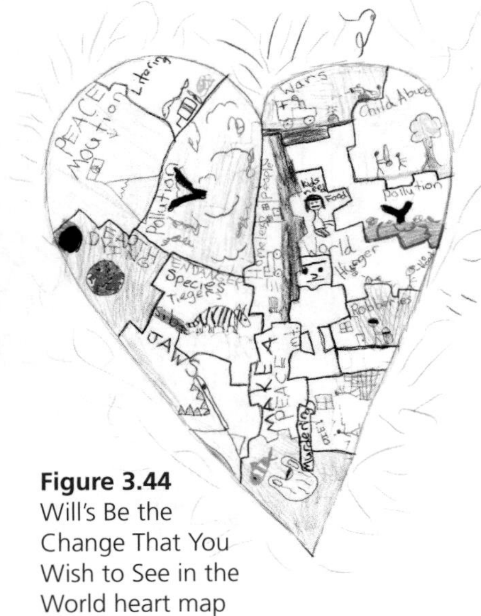

Figure 3.44
Will's Be the Change That You Wish to See in the World heart map

15

A Beloved Character Heart Map

Introduction

I always feel a little heartbroken when I finish reading a book I love. I've become friends with the characters and I feel what they feel, know what they long for, and see through their eyes. Even when I'm not reading their stories every day, they still tug at my heart.

Ellin Keene writes about *character empathy*—one gauge of deep comprehension—"in which we feel we know the characters, experience the same emotions, [and] stand by them in their trials" (2012, 18). Understanding how a character's thoughts and feelings compel his or her actions is part of the key to understanding narrative. Empathizing with a character is what keeps us turning the pages of a book we love.

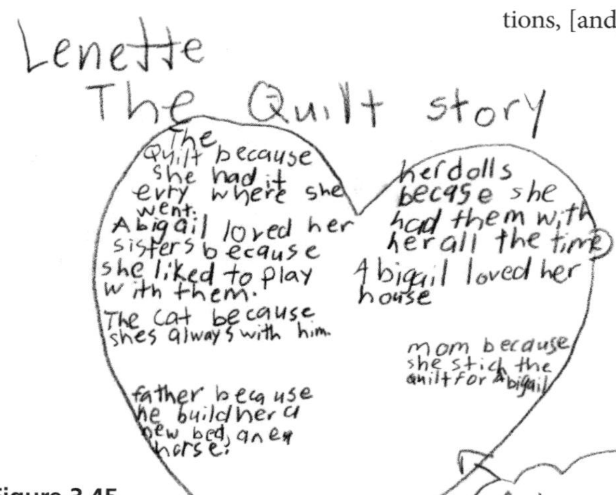

Figure 3.45
Lenette's map of Abigail's heart

Try This

Readers can explore a character's heart by using the Beloved Character Heart Map Template and mapping the character's feelings, thoughts, and reflections: what she loves; what he fears; and what her innermost thoughts and secrets are. We can also map out how we connect to the character. An exploration of a character's emotional life can deepen our understanding of what drives the story as a whole.

Lenette mapped Abigail's heart from *The Quilt Story*, by Tony Johnston (1990), and listed what Abigail loves (see Figure 3.45):

the quilt because she had it everywhere she went

Abigail loved her sisters because she liked to play with them

the cat because she's always with him

father because he built her a new bed and horse

her dolls because she had them with her all the time

Abigail loved her house

Mom because she stitch[ed] the quilt for Abigail

Another reader mapped Helen Keller's heart in *Helen Keller: Courage in the Dark*, by Johanna Hurwitz (1997). The student then took words from the map to form a list poem (see Figure 3.46).

A Beloved Character Heart Map Template

Start by choosing a favorite character from a book you truly love and writing the character's name in the center of your heart map. Here are some questions you might consider as you map:

- What does your character feel at the beginning of the book?
- How do those feelings change?
- What or whom does your character love?
- What is your character afraid of?
- Are there changes in your character? Why?
- What are the places and things she loves?
- What secrets does he keep?
- What are her hopes and dreams?
- What do you have in common with this character?
- What qualities do I see in myself?

Name: ______________________

____

Date: ______________________

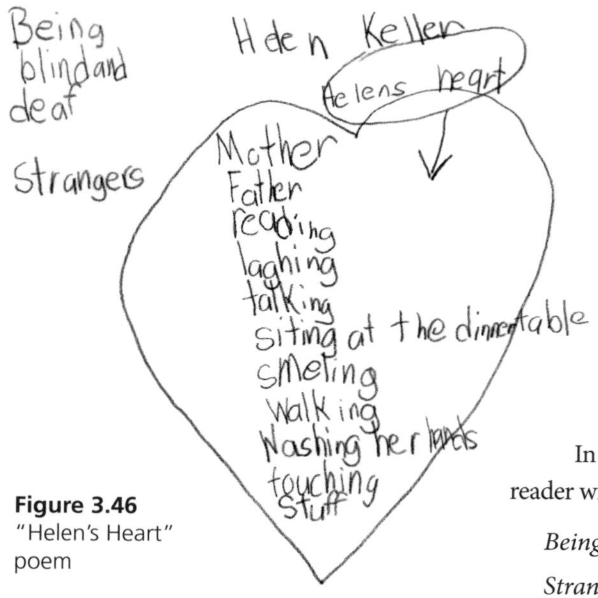

Figure 3.46
"Helen's Heart" poem

Helen's Heart

Mother
Father
Reading
Laughing
Talking
Sitting at the dinner table
Smelling
Walking
Washing her hands
Touching stuff

In the left-hand margin of the heart template, the reader wrote a list of what Helen Keller doesn't love:

Being blind and deaf

Strangers

Readers can also map how a character's feelings change over the course of the book and identify what events lead her to these changes. For example, in Figure 3.47, a reader mapped Maria's feelings in *Too Many Tamales*, by Gary Soto (1996). In squares on the left, the reader identified an event in the story, and then on the right, the reader wrote what the character was feeling. By creating a heart-mapping record of a character's feelings and the events that cause those feelings, readers become aware of how a character's emotions change and what in the narrative causes the changes. For example, on the left, the student wrote, *When Maria is helping her mom make tamales*, and on the right, the reader wrote, *Happy*. But when Maria lost her mother's ring, her feelings changed to *sad*.

The A Beloved Character Heart Map Template represents a mirror that we hold up to see ourselves. We can often connect and understand a character in deep, emotional ways which gives us an empathetic perspective on a book, story, or poem.

Mentor Texts

- Appelt, Kathi. 2010. *The Underneath*. New York: Atheneum Books for Young Readers. (5–9)
- Applegate, Katherine. 2012. *The One and Only Ivan*. New York: HarperCollins Children's Books. (4–6)
- Creech, Sharon. 2011. *Walk Two Moons*. New York: HarperCollins Children's Books. (6–9)

- Draper, Sharon M. 2012. *Out of My Mind*. New York: Atheneum Books for Young Readers. (4–6)
- Hoffman, Mary. 1991. *Amazing Grace*. New York: Dial Books. (Preschool–3)
- Krull, Kathleen. 2000. *Wilma Unlimited: How Wilma Rudolph Became the World's Fastest Woman*. San Diego: Voyager Books. (K–5)
- Ryan, Pam Muñoz. 2002. *Esperanza Rising*. New York: Scholastic. (6–9)
- Spinelli, Jerry. 2002. *Stargirl*. New York: Ember. (7+)
- Woodson, Jacqueline. 2010. *Feathers*. New York: Speak. (4–7)

Writing Ideas

The Beloved Character heart map can support writing personal narrative, literary essay, poetry, and letter writing. Ask students to write a piece using one of these:

- Write a list poem about your character using the words from your heart map. (See "Helen's Heart" in Figure 3.46.)
- Write a personal narrative or literary essay connecting you, your life, and your thoughts and feelings with your character's. Think about these questions: What do you have in common? How is your life similar to or different from your character's? What feelings do you have in common? Does your character help you understand something about yourself that you didn't know before?
- Write a letter to your character telling her or him how you feel and why you feel connected.

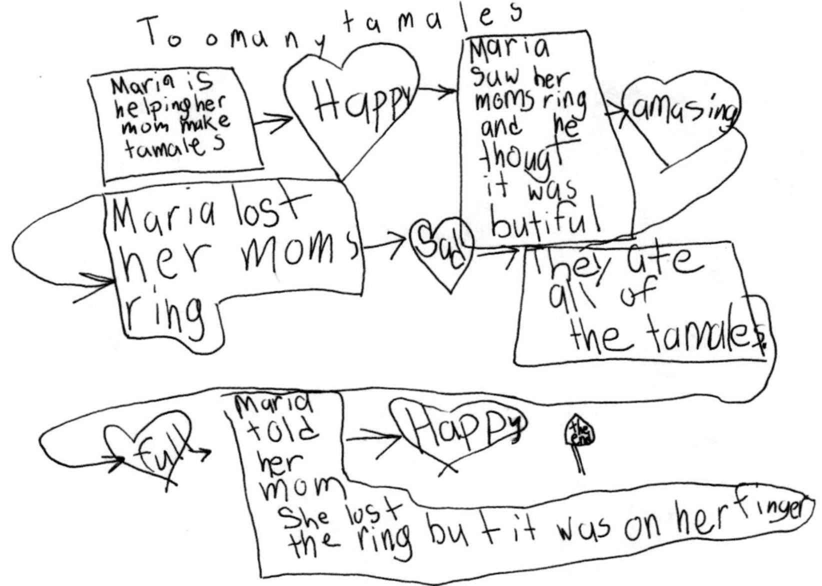

Figure 3.47 Maria's feelings poem

16

People I Admire Heart Map

Introduction

When he researches people for his historical biographies, David McCullough doesn't just ask, "Why is this person famous?" Instead he strives to reach beneath the surface of his subjects' accomplishments to help him (and readers) understand the people more deeply. Speaking in an interview, he explained, "I try to make you see what's happening and smell it and hear it. I want to know what they had for dinner. I want to know how long it took to walk from where to where. . . . What were these people like as human beings?" (2003). These details inform who this person is and go a long way toward giving readers a richer, truer sense of the whole person.

When we write a biography about a person we admire, we want to try to see the world through his or her eyes:

Whom and what does she love?

How does he spend his days?

What secrets does she have?

What makes him laugh?

What are her hopes and dreams?

What is in the heart of this person?

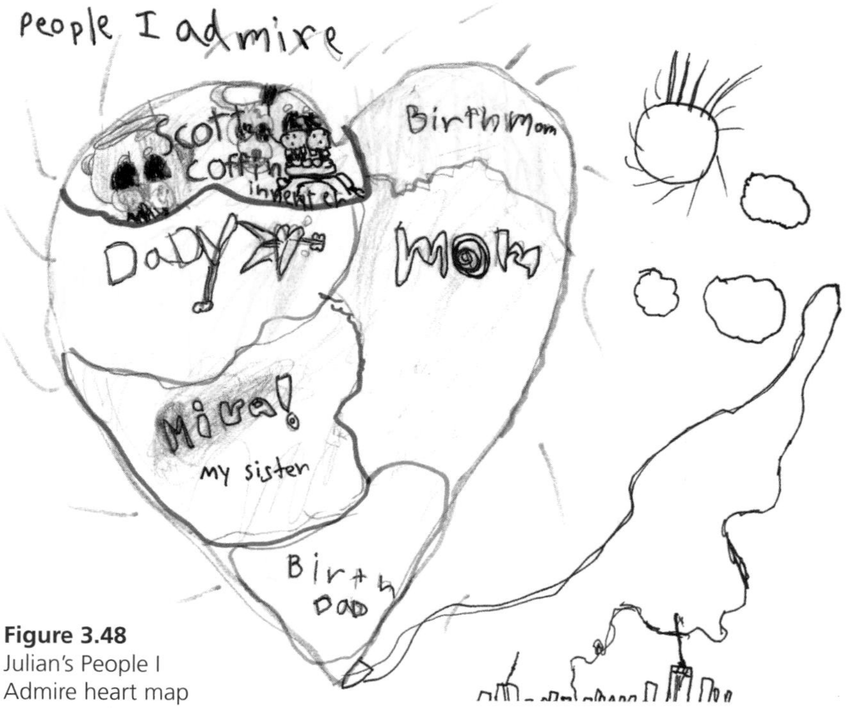

Figure 3.48
Julian's People I Admire heart map

People I Admire Heart Map Template

Write the person or persons you admire in the center of your heart map. Here are some questions to ask yourself as you work:

- What is it about the person that you love or that fascinates you?
- Is there one central trait about the person that is the most interesting?
- What do you wonder about this person's life?
- What are some of the key life experiences and accomplishments that have made this person notable or special?
- What details of the person's life make who he or she is today?
- Is there a surprising trait many people don't know about?

Name: ______________________

____

Date: ______________________

Try This

Writers can map a person or persons they admire using the People I Admire Heart Map Template. They might choose a famous person living now or in history, or an unsung hero: a person they admire in their life. They can explore some of the questions written on the template and also consider a question biographer David McCullough often asked, "What is this person like as a human being?"

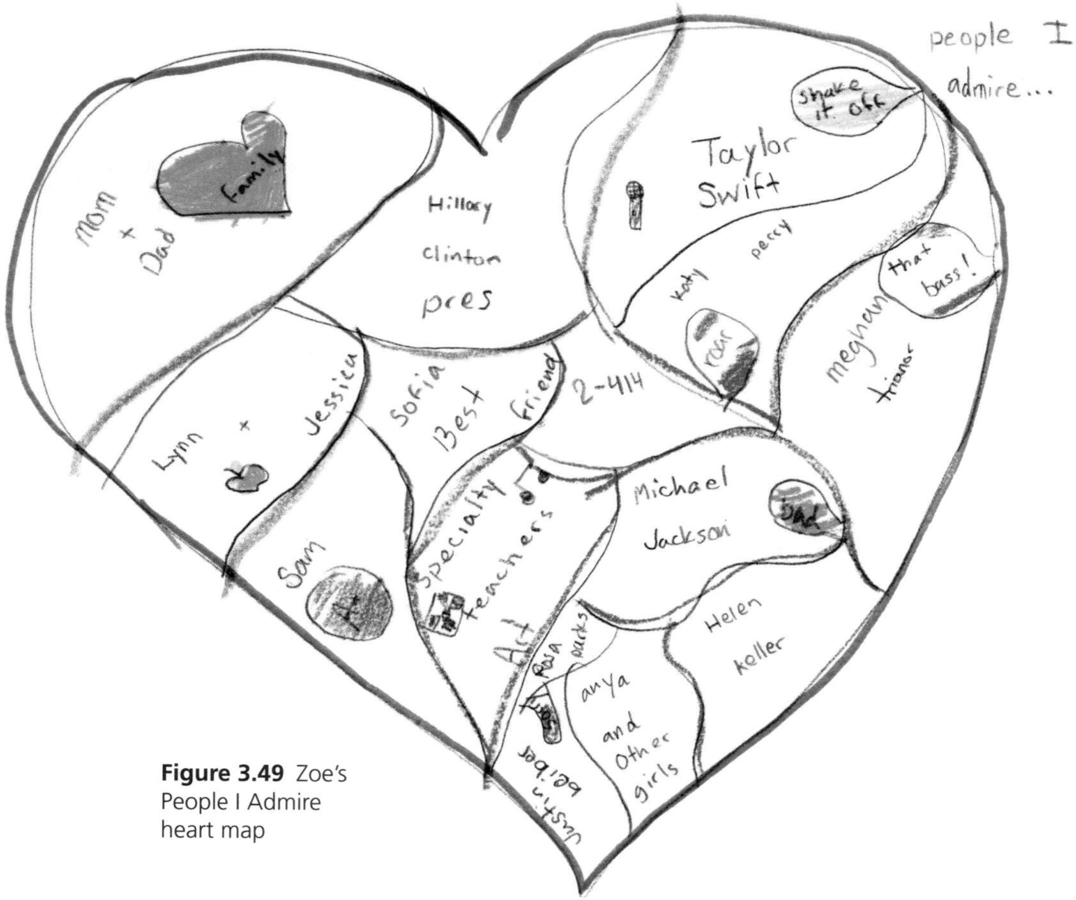

Writing Ideas

The People I Admire heart map can support writing personal narrative, biography, and poetry. Here are some possible activities for students:

- Write a biography of an extraordinary person you admire and choose some of the small moments on your heart map to include in your biography. You might start with the trait you admire the most in the center of your heart map.
- Write a three-line biography of a person you admire, trying to capture the essence of this person in three lines and using some of the words from your heart map. Try not to write facts that we already know about this person. You might have to do some research to find out

Figure 3.49 Zoe's People I Admire heart map

details and information you didn't know before. Here is an example of my three-line biography of Rosa Parks:

She sewed clothes for a living.
Returning from her job on the Cleveland
Authority Bus Line,
she stayed in her seat. Her feet weren't tired.
She was tired of "giving in."

- Write a poem about a person you admire from your heart map and include some of the small, sensory details in your poem. You might begin the poem with what you wrote about the person in the center of your heart.

Mentor Texts

- Barasch, Lynne. 2007. *Hiromi's Hands*. New York: Lee and Low Books. (1+)
- Berne, Jennifer. 2013. *On a Beam of Light: A Story of Albert Einstein*. San Francisco: Chronicle Books. (1–4)
- Chin-Lee, Cynthia. 2005. *Amelia to Zora: Twenty-Six Women Who Changed the World*. Watertown, MA: Charlesbridge. (3–7)
- Engle, Margarita. 2015. *Drum Dream Girl: How One Girl's Courage Changed Music*. New York: HMH Books for Young Readers. (Preschool–3)
- Hopkins, H. Joseph. 2013. *The Tree Lady: The True Story of How One Tree-Loving Woman Changed a City Forever*. New York: Beach Lane Books. (K–5)
- Johnson, Jen Cullerton. 2010. *Seeds of Change: Planting a Path to Peace*. New York: Lee and Low Books. (2+)
- Nazario, Sonia. 2014. *Enrique's Journey: The True Story of a Boy Determined to Reunite with His Mother (Adapted for Young People)*. New York: Ember. (7+)

- Smith, Charles R. Jr. 2015. *28 Days: Moments in Black History That Changed the World*. New York: Roaring Brook Press. (3+)
- Stone, Tanya Lee. 2009. *Almost Astronauts: 13 Women Who Dared to Dream*. Somerville, MA: Candlewick. (5–7)
- Thompson, Laurie Ann. 2015. *Emmanuel's Dream: The True Story of Emmanuel Ofosu Yeboah*. New York: Schwartz and Wade. (Preschool–3)
- Winter, Jeanette. 2011. *The Watcher: Jane Goodall's Life with the Chimps*. New York: Schwartz and Wade Books. (Preschool–3)
- Winter, Jonah. 2009. *Sonia Sotomayor: A Judge Grows in the Bronx/La juez que creció en el Bronx*. New York: Atheneum Books for Young Readers. (Preschool–3)

17

Where I Find Poetry Heart Map

Introduction

Poets find poems everywhere. We try to sharpen both our inner and outer vision to find poems. If we look only *out*, our poems will have no heart, and if we look only *in*, our poems won't be rooted in the detail that keeps them from becoming vague and inaccessible.

In my poem "Where I Find Poetry," I write about looking at the world with a poet's eyes, using both outer and inner vision to observe the world around me (Heard and Laminack 2007, 6.)

Where I Find Poetry

I open my eyes and what do I see?
Poetry spinning all around me!

In small ants trailing over the ground,
Bulldozing dry earth into cave and mound.

In a hundred grains of ocean sand,
that I cradle in the palm of my hand.

In a lullaby of April rain,
tapping softly on my window pane.

In trees dancing on a windy day,
when sky is wrinkled and elephant gray.

Poetry, *poetry!* Can be found
in, out and all around.

But take a look inside your heart,
that's where a poem truly likes to start.

Try This

Students can use the Where I Find Poetry Heart Map Template to find poetry in the world around them. The template shows a poet's path, with a star to begin and an *x* to end the search to find poetry. Writers can also go for a poetry walk and absorb the sights and sounds around them. When they return from their walk, they can map their heart with the sights and sounds they noticed. Remind them to write small—instead of simply writing, *I see trees*, they might write *trees dancing on a windy day.* Encourage writers to use all their senses to describe details.

Figure 3.50 Alexx's Where I Find Poetry heart map

Where I Find Poetry Heart Map Template

Use the Where I Find Poetry Heart Map Template to map the amazing and beautiful world around you to inspire possible poems:

- everyday observations
- beautiful and awe-inspiring people, places, and things
- small things and moments that almost pass us by
- stories and memories that you've stored in your heart
- anything that makes you feel strongly.

Name: ______________________

____

Date: ______________________

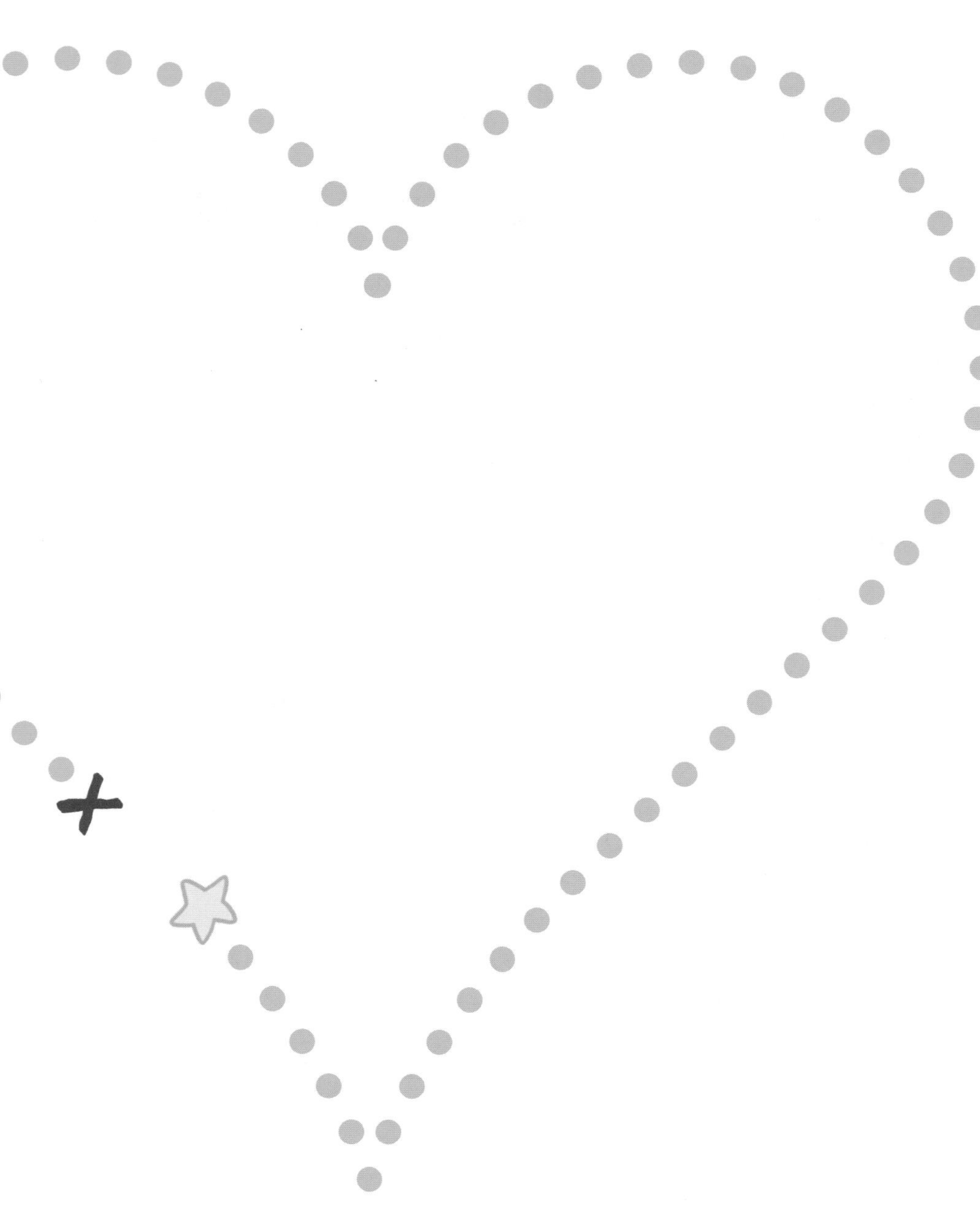

Writing Ideas

The Where I Find Poetry heart map supports writing poetry. Encourage writers to try one of these poetry-writing invitations:

- Write a list poem listing a few of the memorable things you wrote on your heart map. Think about how you will end the poem—a few options are ending with a surprise image; summing up the places where you find poetry; or repeating a line or word from earlier in the poem. (See *Falling Down the Page: A Book of List Poems* [Heard 2011] for inspiration.)
- Close your eyes and make a mental movie in your mind of one thing you wrote on your heart map. Then describe the movie using words. Write it in poetry form using line breaks and stanzas.
- After your poetry walk, start your poem with the line *I open my eyes and what do I see?* Then select those entries on your heart map that are the most memorable, cracking open words that are not concrete. For example, instead of writing *ants* in "Where Do I Find Poetry?" I cracked open the word and included details I observed about ants: "In small ants trailing over the ground, / bulldozing dry earth into cave and mound. . . ."
- Transform a story you've already written, or one you have in your mind, into a novel in verse (read *The Crossover* by Kwame Alexander in the mentor text list that follows).
- Using *The Arrow Finds Its Mark: A Book of Found Poems* (see list of mentor texts) as a mentor text, gather print from magazines, newspapers, signs, and so on to create a Found Poem.

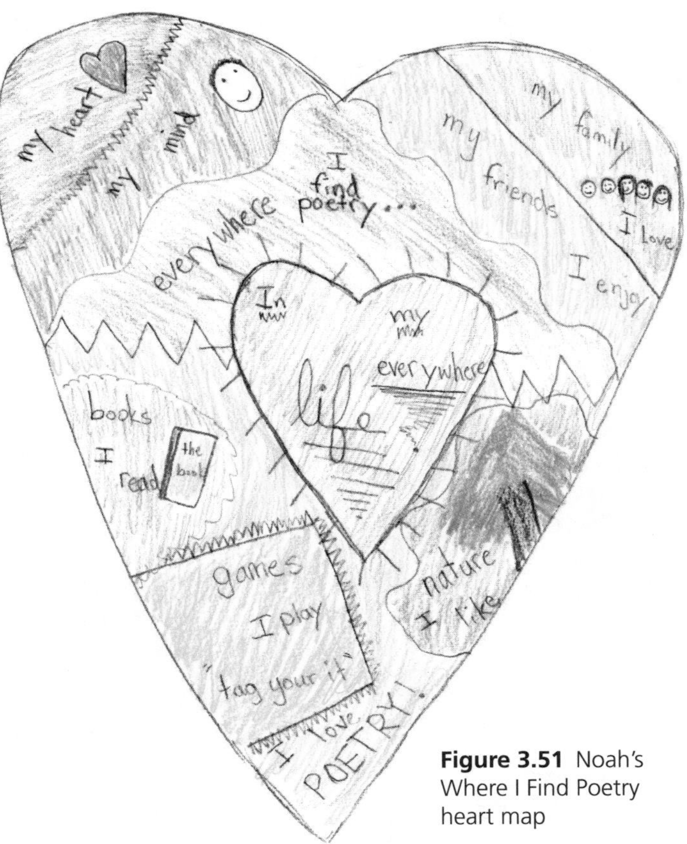

Figure 3.51 Noah's Where I Find Poetry heart map

Mentor Texts

- Alarcón, Francisco X. 2005. *Laughing Tomatoes and Other Spring Poems*. New York: Children's Book Press. (1–5)
- Alexander, Kwame. 2014. *The Crossover*. Boston: HMH Books for Young Readers. (5–7)
- Archer, Micha. 2016. *Daniel Finds a Poem*. New York: Nancy Paulsen Books. (K+)
- Dotlich, Rebecca Kai. 2001. *Lemonade Sun: And Other Summer Poems*. Honesdale, PA: WordSong. (1–3)
- ———. 2009. *Bella and Bean*. New York: Atheneum Books for Young Readers. (Preschool–3)
- Heard, Georgia, ed. 2011. *Falling Down the Page: A Book of List Poems*. New York: Square Fish. (3+)
- ———. 2012. *The Arrow Finds Its Mark: A Book of Found Poems*. New York: Roaring Brook. (3–6)
- Holbrook, Sara. 2003. *By Definition: Poems of Feelings*. Honesdale, PA: WordSong. (4–7)
- Hopkins, Lee Bennett. 2016. *Nasty Bugs*. New York: Puffin Books. (1–3)
- Janeczko, Paul. 2014. *Firefly July: A Year of Very Short Poems*. Somerville, MA: Candlewick. (1–4)
- Kousky, Vern. 2015. *Otto the Owl Who Loved Poetry*. New York: Nancy Paulsen Books. (K–3)
- Lewis, Patrick J. 2014. *Everything Is a Poem: The Best of J. Patrick Lewis*. North Mankato, MN: Creative Editions. (1–3)
- McNamara, Margaret. 2015. *A Poem in Your Pocket*. New York: Schwartz and Wade. (Preschool–3)
- Nye, Naomi Shihab. 2005. *A Maze Me: Poems for Girls*. New York: Greenwillow Books. (8–11)

- Paulsen, Gary. 2001. *Canoe Days*. New York: Dragonfly Books. (Preschool–2)
- Sidman, Joyce. 2014. *Winter Bees and Other Poems of the Cold*. Boston: Houghton Mifflin Harcourt. (K–4)
- Singer, Marilyn. 2010. *Mirror Mirror: A Book of Reverso Poems*. New York: Dutton Books for Young Readers. (1–4)
- VanDerwater, Amy Ludwig. 2013. *Forest Has a Song: Poems*. Boston: Clarion Books. (1–4)
- Vardell, Sylvia, and Janet Wong, eds. 2012. *The Poetry Friday Anthology: Poems for the School Year with Connections to the Common Core, K–5 Edition*. Princeton, NJ: Pomelo Books. (K–5)

Poetry

- Collins, Billy. 1988. "Introduction to Poetry." In *The Apple That Astonished Paris*. Fayetteville: University of Arkansas Press. (6+)
- Herrera, Juan Felipe. 2008. "Let Me Tell You What a Poem Brings." In *Half of the World in Light: New and Selected Poems*. Tucson: University of Arizona Press. (7+)
- Koriyama, Naoshi. 1957. "Unfolding Bud." *Christian Science Monitor*, July 13. (2+)
- Nye, Naomi Shihab. 1994. "Valentine for Earnest Mann." In *Red Suitcase*, 70–71. Rochester, NY: BOA Editions. (2+)

For high school students, share some of Sarah Kay's spoken word poetry, which can be found on her website at www.kaysarahsera.com/videos. You can also explore the following sites for inspirational poems:

http://poetryfoundation.org/

https://www.poets.org

http://poetryoutloud.org

18

Senses Heart Map

Introduction

Senses are doorways into writing. Our senses allow writers to experience the world around us, and they are the windows through which readers experience the worlds we create. Lee Martin (2012) writes, "So much of the work of [writing] is done on the seemingly small scale of what things look like, smell like, sound like, taste like, feel like." If I try to write without using sensory imagery, my writing becomes dry and abstract. The simple act of paying attention to what you notice—not only with your eyes, but with all of the ways you experience the sensory world—offers up a bounty of detail and breathes life into your writing.

Try This

Writers can use the Senses Heart Map Template to map out sensory details of a moment, memory, experience, person, or other topic. The template evokes the sense of touch with its pointy, sharp peaks, as well as the ebb and flow of sound. Remind writers that no matter the genre, sensory description creates a world that the reader can experience, and that description is not just to make us see and hear, etc., but to help us feel.

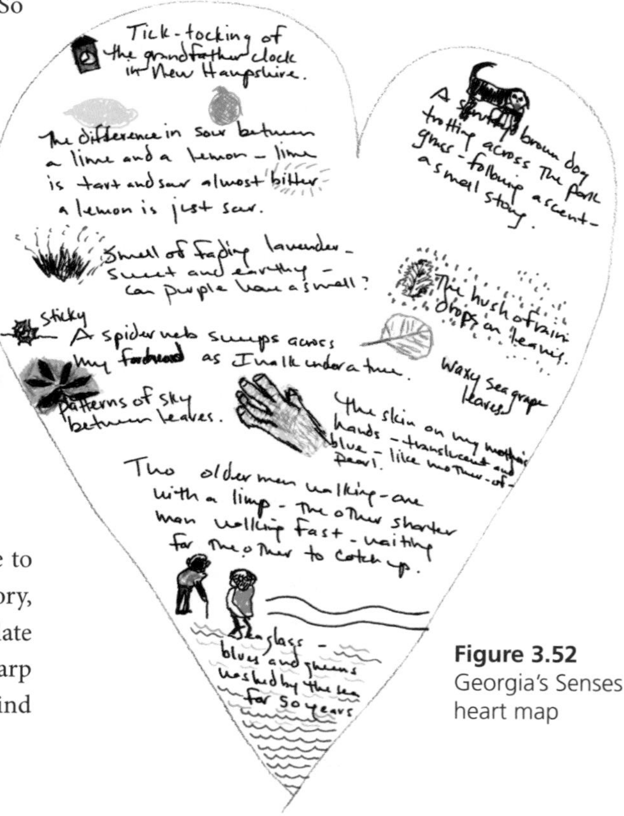

Figure 3.52
Georgia's Senses heart map

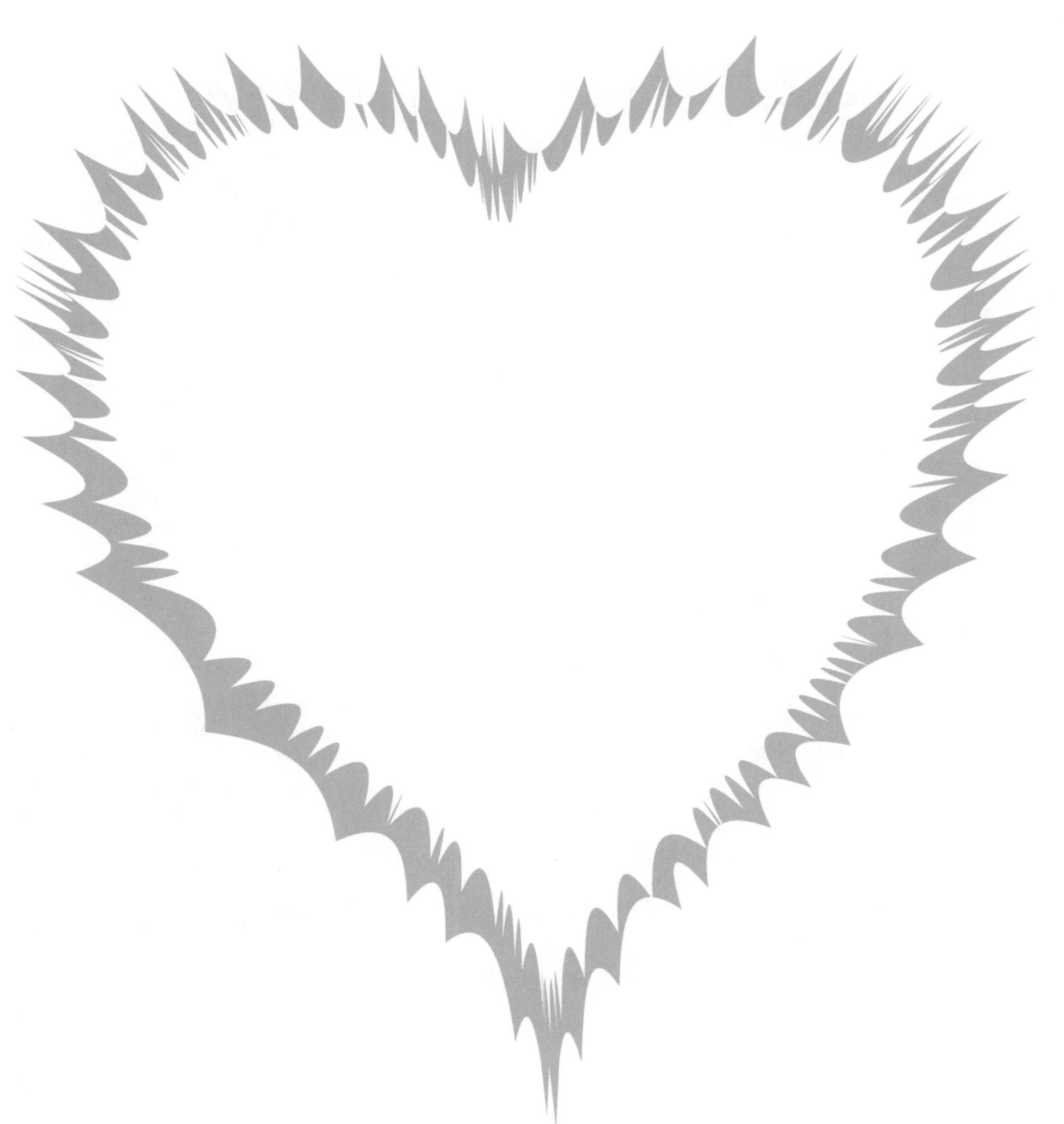

Senses Heart Map Template

Use the Senses Heart Map Template to fill your heart with sensory details—the sights, smells, sounds, tastes, and textures of your childhood, your home, your world.

- Observe a moment and make a movie in your mind. What do you see? Map visual details such as colors, lights, and shadows.
- Map aural (sound) details, like listening to music or the sound of someone's voice.
- Map smells, like the smell of cooking or a fragrance that reminds you of someone you love.
- Map the sense of touch and describe the texture of something.
- Or you might want to highlight one sense and fill your heart map with details from the world around you using only that one sense.

Name: ______________________

____

Date: ______________________

Writing Ideas

A Senses heart map will support writing in all genres. Give writers one of the following prompts to get them started:

- Write a poem using only sensory details from your heart map. Focus on one sense at a time, or mix the senses together. Try not to make any statements in the poem like what the poem is about; use only details to show. Write the larger meaning of the poem as a title.
- Write a paragraph in a personal narrative and focus in on one sense at a time in your description.
- Write a sensory memoir with each chapter highlighting details one sense at a time.
- Write a nonfiction informational piece focusing on sensory details from your heart map. As you research your topic, gather information and facts that emphasize sensory details and include them on your heart map.
- Write a personal or descriptive essay focusing on how you perceive the world with one sense.

Mentor Texts

- Aston, Dianna Hutts. 2015. *A Nest Is Noisy*. San Francisco: Chronicle Books. (K–3)
- Gorrell, Nancy. 1997. "Blueberry Pie." In *Reflections on a Gift of Watermelon Pickle . . . and Other Modern Verse*, 2d edition, edited by Stephen Dunning, Edward Lueders, and Hugh Smith, X[0]. Boston: Addison Wesley. (6+)
- Grandin, Temple. 2006. "Seeing in Beautiful, Precise Pictures." *This I Believe* (blog). http://thisibelieve.org/essay/18/. (7+)
- Moore, Lilian. 2013. *Mural on Second Avenue and Other City Poems*. Cambridge, MA: Candlewick. (K–4)
- McCloskey, Robert. 1989. *Time of Wonder*. New York: Puffin Books. (Preschool–2)
- Paulsen, Gary. 2001. *Canoe Days*. New York: Dragonfly Books. (Preschool–2)

- Seeger, Laura Vaccaro. 2012. *Green*. New York: Roaring Brook Press. (Preschool–1)
- Sidman, Joyce. 2005. *Song of the Water Boatman: And Other Pond Poems*. Boston: HMH Books for Young Readers. (Preschool–3)
- ———. 2009. *Red Sings from Treetops: A Year in Colors*. Boston: HMH Books for Young Readers. (Preschool–3)
- VanDerwater, Amy Ludwig. 2013. *Forest Has a Song: Poems*. Boston: Clarion Books. (1–4)
- Yolen, Jane. 2003. *Color Me a Rhyme: Nature Poems for Young People*. Honesdale, PA: WordSong. (3–6)

Students in grades 4 and above may also appreciate the imagery in the lyrics of John Mayer's song "3×5" on the 2001 album *Room for Squares* (Sony Music Entertainment).

19

Nonfiction Heart Maps

Introduction

When I was going to school, nonfiction writing consisted of the teacher assigning a topic and the class looking it up in the encyclopedia the night before it was due to copy information, making sure to delete a few *ands* so we wouldn't get arrested for plagiarism.

Heart mapping can guide writers in finding nonfiction topics that they're passionate about, giving purpose to the craft work they will do once they begin to write. (My book *Finding the Heart of Nonfiction: Teaching 7 Essential Craft Tools with Mentor Texts* [2013] discusses seven essential nonfiction craft tools that will help writers in genres of nonfiction.)

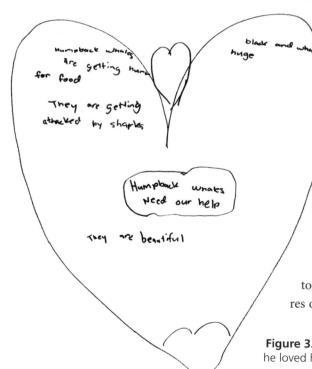

Figure 3.53 Grayson's heart map on why he loved humpback whales

Nonfiction writers can map their hearts to explore topics in science, social studies, and history or to generate ideas for book reviews and personal, opinion, and persuasive essays. Writers who have chosen topics can heart map to identify a focus, and writers who are still searching for a topic can heart map to explore.

We don't use the word *love* often in schools today, especially when referring to nonfiction writing, but without passion and enthusiasm, nonfiction writing can become mechanical and dull—just another assignment to complete. Perhaps we need to revise the widespread brainstorming tool K–W–L, which illustrates what a student *knows*, *wonders*, and *learns*, to K–W–L–L, with the final *L* representing what a student *loves*.

Try This

Nonfiction writing is often a dance between what the writer knows and what they don't know, and through research, we walk through unexpected doorways that lead to answers, and even more doorways. Students can use one of two Nonfiction Heart Map Templates to guide their nonfiction journey. The Nonfiction Heart

Nonfiction Heart Map: Finding Your Topic Template

As you map your heart to find a nonfiction topic, include some of the following ideas:

- What are you an expert at or what do you know a lot about?
- What are some of the things you notice and pay close attention to in the world?
- What do you wonder about?
- What do you want to learn more about?
- What are you amazed at?
- What have you heard, noticed, or read lately that surprised or interested you?

Name: ______________________

____

Date: ______________________

Nonfiction Heart Map: Exploring Your Topic Template

When you know what your nonfiction topic is then include some of the following on your heart map:

- Write what you love most about your topic. (You might want to place that in the center of your heart map.)
- What are some of the reasons you love your topic (personal observation, wonder, or memory?
- What really fascinates you about your topic?
- When and how you began to love your topic.
- If your topic is something you have observed personally, map your observation and what it was about that observation that stuck with you.
- What are some specific facts and information that you know about your topic that have inspired your interest?

Name: ______________________

____

Date: ______________________

Map: Finding Your Topic Template is a heart magnifying glass representing the process of looking closely at the world to find a nonfiction topic that matters. The second, Nonfiction Heart Map: Exploring Your Topic Template, is a heart with a maze around the edge to symbolize the exploration of a topic students know they want to write about that will include the false starts and backtracking that nonfiction writers often encounter on their travels of exploring a topic.

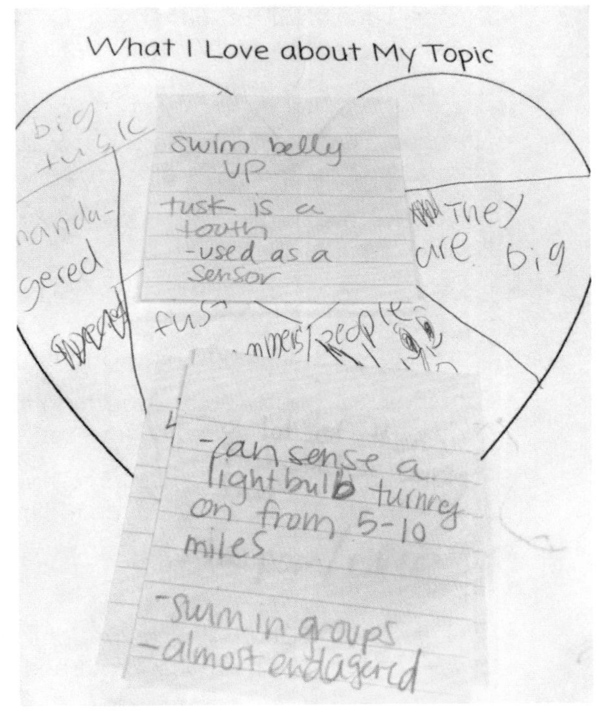

Figure 3.54 After researching his topic about narwhals, Will added more reasons he loved his topic on sticky notes.

Writing Ideas

The Nonfiction Heart Maps will support writing in various genres of nonfiction, such as reports or articles in science, social studies, and history; book reviews; and personal, opinion, and persuasive essays.

Mentor Texts

- Aronson, Marc, and Marina Budhos. 2010. *Sugar Changed the World: A Story of Magic, Spice, Slavery, Freedom, and Science*. Boston: Clarion Books. (8+)
- Aston, Dianna Hutts. 2007. *A Seed Is Sleepy*. San Francisco: Chronicle Books. (1–4)
- Butterworth, Chris. 2009. *Sea Horse: The Shyest Fish in the Sea*. Cambridge, MA: Candlewick. (Preschool–3)

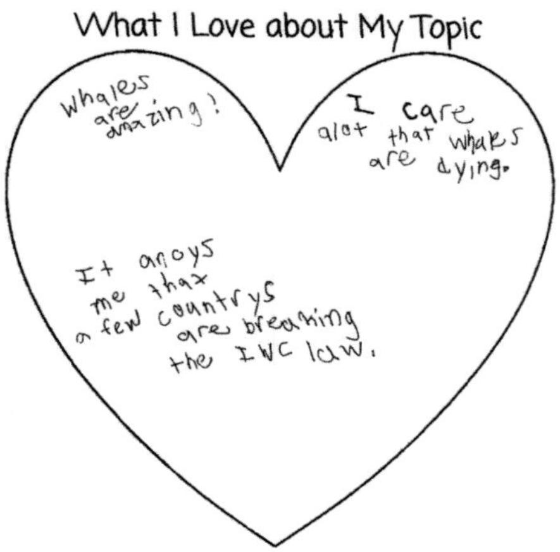

What I Love about My Topic

Figure 3.55 Evan wrote what he loved about his topic, which was also humpback whales.

- Davies, Nicola. 2001a. *Bat Loves the Night*. Cambridge, MA: Candlewick. (K–4)
- ———. 2001b. *Big Blue Whale*. Cambridge, MA: Candlewick. (K–3)
- Harrison, David L. 2016. *Now You See Them, Now You Don't: Poems About Creatures That Hide*. Watertown, MA: Charlesbridge. (K–4)
- Jenkins, Steve. 2014. *Eye to Eye: How Animals See the World*. Boston: HMH Books for Young Readers. (1–4)
- Lewis, J. Patrick, ed. 2015. *National Geographic Book of Nature Poetry: More than 200 Poems with Photographs That Float, Zoom, and Bloom!* Washington, DC: National Geographic Children's Books. (K–4)
- Partridge, Elizabeth. 2009. *Marching for Freedom: Walk Together, Children, and Don't You Grow Weary*. New York: Viking Juvenile. (6–12)
- Pringle, Laurence. 2011. *Billions of Years, Amazing Changes: The Story of Evolution*. Honesdale, PA: Boyds Mills. (3+)
- Stewart, Melissa. 2014. *Feathers: Not Just for Flying*. Watertown, MA: Charlesbridge. (1–4)
- Walker, Sally M. 2009. *Written in Bone: Buried Lives of Jamestown and Colonial Maryland*. Minneapolis: Carolrhoda Books. (6–9)

Another good resource for grades 4–7 is the Take a Walk series, published by Stillwater.

20

What I Wonder About Heart Map

Introduction

In a SuperSoul Session, author Elizabeth Gilbert makes a case for a curiosity-driven life: "It gives you permission to go on a kind of perpetual scavenger hunt searching for clues, asking and answering questions" (www.supersoul.tv/supersoul-sessions/elizabeth-gilbert-flight-hummingbird-curiosity). All children share this kind of enthusiasm and curiosity about the world, and it is our responsibility to notice and nurture that trait. Writing is like a scavenger hunt as we search for meaningful topics, look for just the right words, and seek clarity, all the while aiming for the heart of our writing.

Bret Anthony Johnston (2011) tells his Harvard University writing students to write about what they don't know. He says that all his life, he heard the advice *Write what you know*, but he realized that following that path led him "to explain, not to discover." He continues, "The writing process was as exciting as completing a crossword puzzle I'd already solved. So I changed my approach." Using what we don't know as a starting point can bring the marvelous energy of curiosity into our writing.

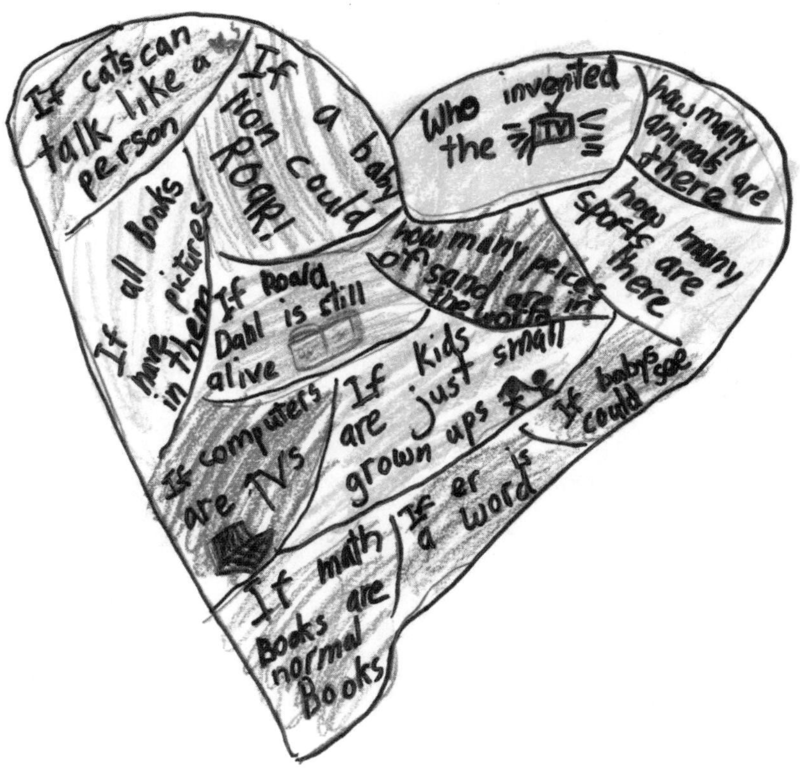

Figure 3.56 Luciana's What I Wonder About heart map

What I Wonder About Heart Map Template

Use the What I Wonder About Heart Map Template to explore and write what you don't know. As you work, ask yourself:

- What do I wonder about in my life, the world, what I'm studying in school?
- What do I want to know more about?
- Is there one wonder above all others that I can place at the center of my heart?
- Are there questions that I've had for a long time or that keep me up at night?

Name: ______________________

____

Date: ______________________

Try This

Writers can use the What I Wonder About Heart Map Template to write what they don't know—questions they have about their lives, the world, what they're studying in school, things they read about that interest them, and ideas that keep them up at night. The two halves of the heart form two question marks that invite writers to explore their wonders, curiosities, observations, thoughts, and reflections.

Writing Ideas

A What I Wonder About heart map can support writing in multiple genres. Ask students to respond to one of the following:

- Read your What I Wonder About heart map to see which wonders spark a poem, nonfiction, essay, or personal narrative.
- Gather your wonders from your heart map and arrange them in an "I Wonder" poem.
- For a nonfiction informational piece, let your wonders guide your research about one topic, as they did for one third grader in his nonfiction informational heart map on loggerhead turtles (see Figure 3.57).

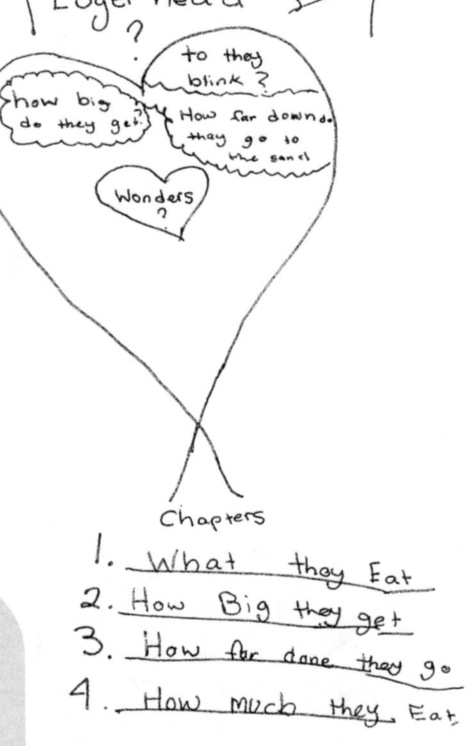

Figure 3.57 What I Wonder About heart map on loggerhead turtles

Mentor Texts

- Cobb, Vicki. 2010. *What's the Big Idea? Amazing Science Questions for the Curious Kid*. New York: Skyhorse. (3–6)
- Curtis, Jamie Lee. 2000. *Where Do Balloons Go? An Uplifting Mystery*. New York: HarperCollins. (Preschool–3)
- Ganeri, Anita. 2003. *I Wonder Why the Sea Is Salty and Other Questions About the Oceans*. New York: Kingfisher. (K–3)
- Harris, Gemma Elwin, compiler. 2012. *Big Questions from Little People—and Simple Answers from Great Minds*. New York: Ecco. (3–7)
- Kochanoff, Peggy. 2009. *You Can Be a Nature Detective*. Missoula, MT: Mountain Press. (3+)

- Kuefler, Joseph. 2015. *Beyond the Pond*. New York: Balzer and Bray. (Preschool–3)
- Merriam, Eve. 1991. *The Wise Woman and Her Secret*. New York: Simon and Schuster. (1–2)
- Pfister, Marcus. 2011. *Questions, Questions*. New York: NorthSouth. (Preschool–2)
- Roemer, Heidi Bee. 2009. *Whose Nest Is This?* Lanham, MD: NorthWord. (Preschool–3)
- Sisson, Stephanie Roth. 2014. *Star Stuff: Carl Sagan and the Mysteries of the Cosmos*. New York: Roaring Brook. (Preschool–3)
- Waber, Bernard. 2015. *Ask Me*. Boston: HMH Books for Young Readers. (Preschool–3)

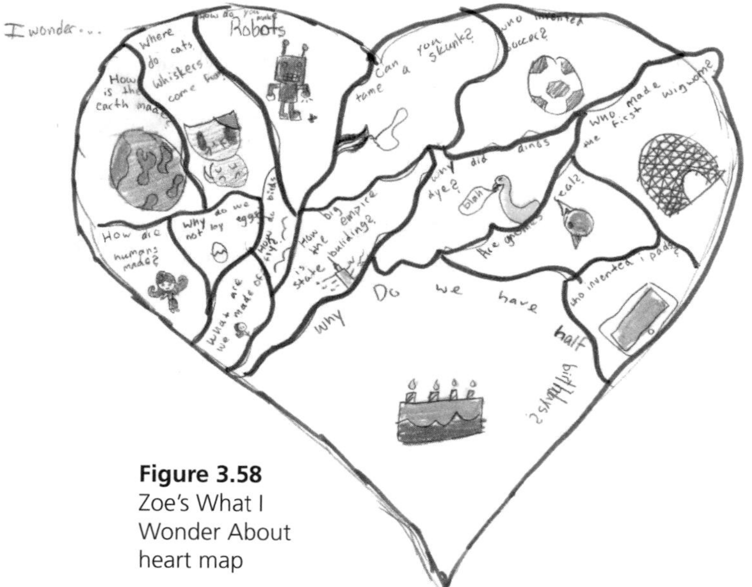

Figure 3.58
Zoe's What I Wonder About heart map

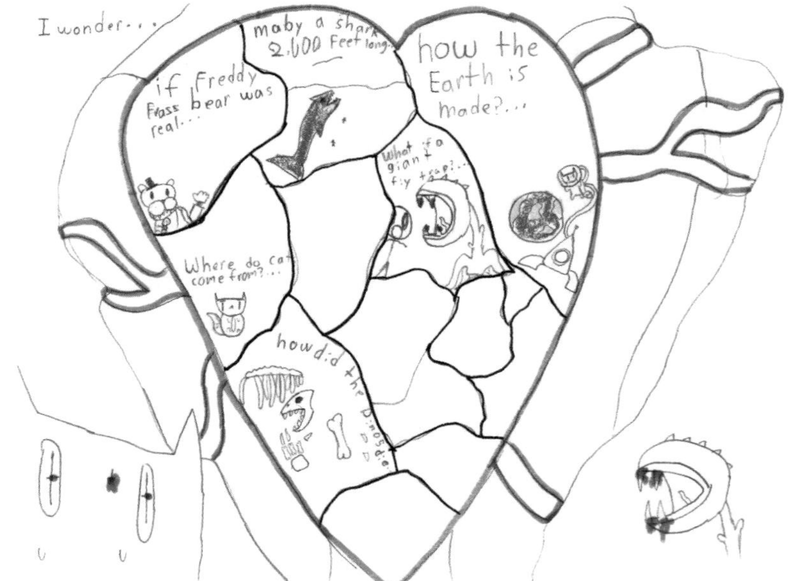

Figure 3.59
Rumi's What I Wonder About heart map

Digging Deeper into Heart Maps

Sharing, Reflecting on, and Writing from Heart Maps

Heart maps are beautiful works of art in themselves. In fact, someday I'd like to gather a collection from all over the world for an art exhibit so people can view all the beauty that lies in children's hearts. The process of heart mapping is deep and honest personal work. But there are layers of stories and feelings that we can't immediately see when we first look at a heart map. Words and drawings can sometimes be place markers, begging writers to return and go deeper by sharing, talking, reflecting, and writing. If we could whisper to writers' heart maps, we would say, "Tell me *more*."

When we pull up Google Maps and click on a plus sign to zoom in on a map, suddenly everything comes into crystal-clear focus. What started out as a generic map is now a unique town filled with trees, parks, street names, and stores. We can almost begin to hear the conversations on a street, or see a dog trotting along a sidewalk, or see a child licking an ice-cream cone.

Similarly, when we zoom in on our heart maps, the details of our stories come into focus. For example, the word *pets* becomes a house full of cats with funny names, or *family* becomes the ritual of bedtime stories your grandmother tells you.

This chapter is about zooming in, stretching out, and digging deep into the inner terrain of heart maps.

Sharing Heart Maps

Heart mapping can bring up a lot of powerful feelings and memories, so be sure to build in time for sharing immediately after heart mapping. Students can place their heart maps on a document camera or a desktop easel so all the children can see the heart map, and to make it easier to share details in their heart maps. In addition to sharing with a large group, writers can share with a paired partner or in small groups. Ask writers to choose one or two key

The idea is to write it so that people hear it and it slides through the brain and goes straight to the heart.

—Maya Angelou

Tip: Heart maps are not meant to function simply as topic lists; we don't expect writers to tackle and check off every single entry as they go. Heart mapping is a means of paying attention, opening oneself to writing possibilities. Just as not every notebook entry will turn into a longer piece of writing, not every heart map entry will kindle new writing.

Ryan, a student in Mary Glover's class at the wonderful Awakening Seed School, wrote this simple yet wise statement about reading his heart map to find writing topics: *I really liked looking deeper in my heart and finding what I really liked.*

parts of their heart maps to share. They can also tell anything new or surprising that they discovered about themselves, or they can discuss what the process of heart mapping was like for them.

Listeners can respond in constructive ways with comments and questions such as these:

- I really like this part of your heart map.
- What is the most important part of your heart map?
- What does ______ mean?
- Can you say more about that part?
- I felt the same way and wrote something similar on my heart map.

Sharing heart maps is beneficial in so many ways. It can help students

- empathize and connect with one another
- feel less alone
- realize the abundance of stories and writing ideas inside them
- gain confidence
- know how full their hearts are
- become better listeners
- have meaningful conversations with each other
- share beliefs and ideas that matter to them
- bond with a classroom community in deep ways.

One of my favorite poems about being a good listener in life and also as a writer is "When Someone Deeply Listens to You," by John Fox (1997):

When Someone Deeply Listens to You

When someone deeply listens to you
it is like holding out a dented cup
you've had since childhood
and watching it fill up with
cold, fresh water.
When it balances on top of the brim,
you are understood.
When it overflows and touches your skin,
you are loved.

When someone deeply listens to you
the room where you stay
starts a new life
and the place where you wrote
your first poem
begins to glow in your mind's eye.
It is as if gold has been discovered!

When someone deeply listens to you
your barefeet are on the earth
and a beloved land that seemed distant
is now at home within you.

As teachers, we want to model being good listeners who make every student feel understood, inspiring each writer to take risks and honestly share.

Writing from Heart Maps

A heart map can be a well that the writer draws from for writing ideas throughout the entire year. Mary Glover, teacher extraordinaire and founder of the

Awakening Seed School in Phoenix, Arizona, offers wise advice: "We did a group map first and then moved right into doing their individual maps. It seemed important that they understood and practiced the process of making the map first before beginning to use it as a tool for finding topics to write about."

Start by sharing not only your own heart map but also your process of rereading and selecting writing topics from your heart map by asking, "Which entries on my heart map could I expand into a longer piece of writing?" On a chart, jot down a list of writing ideas. As you write your list, make a note of what genre you think might work best for each idea.

When conferring, you might guide young writers to explore some of the following ideas and questions:

- As you look over your heart map, scan for parts that resonate for you emotionally; tell a story that begs to be written; or express a feeling that tugs at your heart.
- To get started writing, place your writer's notebook beside your heart map, or take a blank sheet of paper, and freewrite the thoughts, feelings, and images that emerge. You might also create a topic list of writing ideas from your heart map for later use.
- Ask yourself what genre fits the idea you've chosen best: A poem? A small moment or personal narrative? An essay? Or another genre?

Revising Writing from Heart Maps

For me, revision is rewriting until what I write feels truthful, complete, and alive. This usually means dozens of drafts. I match what's in my heart and mind with the words I've written until the match is as perfect as I can make it. When writers measure what's in their hearts and minds against what they've written, they can ask:

> Where does the writing feel the same as what I hold in my heart and mind?
>
> Where does the writing not feel authentic and is not what I wanted to express?
>
> Why, how, and where do the parts feel not quite right?

One of the heart-mapping revision strategies I suggest to students is to make a heart map of their narrative, poem, or essay using the Heart of My Writing Heart Map Template (see p. 112).

Mimi, a third grader, originally wrote details about kayaking in her heart map, but when she reflected on her story, she realized that the heart of her story was *kayaking by herself*. As she wrote her personal narrative, and fleshed out details, she kept that focus in mind and let it guide her (see Figure 4.1).

Prior to writing, and as writers draft, they can refer back to the heart map to help them keep a piece focused. Writers can ask themselves questions such as these:

Writing Genres Supported by Heart Maps

A heart map holds so many stories and ideas that beg for telling, whether it be in poem form, memoir, personal narrative, or some other genre.

How do writers decide what genre fits best?

Sometimes your class might be engaged in studying a particular genre in writing workshop, so the writing will, of course, tend to fit with that study. Sometimes a particular topic pulls a writer toward a certain genre. And sometimes a writer loves to write in a certain genre and tends to choose that one.

At the end of each heart map description in Chapter 3 there are writing ideas, including which genres each heart map might best support.

The Heart of My Writing Heart Map Template

Prior to writing, and as you draft your writing, go deeper into your topic and ask yourself and map the following questions:

- What is the heart of my piece?
- What are some of the details that will elaborate the heart of my piece?

Name: ______________________

____

Date: ______________________

- What is the heart of my piece?
- What are some of the details that will elaborate the heart of my piece?

Real revision is inner work: clarifying what we really think and believe about an idea; getting at the heart of a story; distilling our sentences and words to best express how we feel and what we think. As Rilke wrote, "Work of the eyes is done, now / Go and do heart-work" (1989, 133–4).

Using Mentor Texts with Heart Maps

When I'm working on a piece of writing, I often immerse myself in the words of my favorite writers, letting them wash over me. Something magical happens when I read alongside my writing—it's as though the rhythms and patterns of my mentors find their way into my own voice, allowing me to try new things and showing me possibilities. Reading powerful writing can inspire and warm writers up. Each heart map section in Chapter 3 is accompanied by a relevant list of mentor texts in multiple genres.

Here are some ways to use mentor texts with heart maps:

- Read several mentor texts aloud and let the words wash over writers. Savor and celebrate the words. Invite writers to point out what they love about what they've heard.
- Collect mentor texts in small packets to accompany a particular kind of heart map. Writers can independently read, follow the links for, and study these mentor texts for craft ideas as they begin to write from their own heart maps.
- Show writers' craft moves from mentor texts during writing minilessons related to the kinds of writing students will be doing from heart mapping.

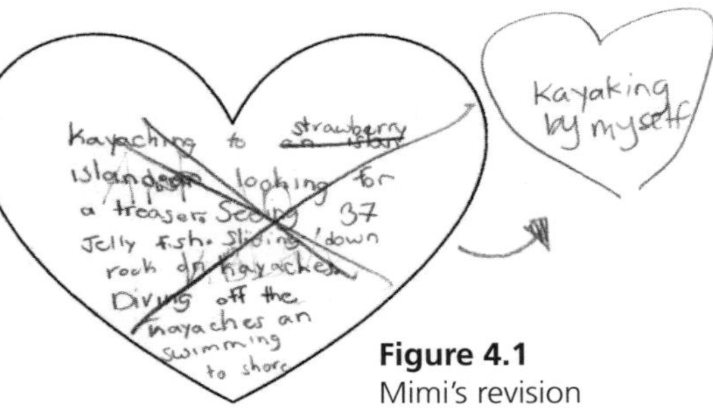

Figure 4.1
Mimi's revision

Reflecting on Using Heart Maps to Support Writing

In addition to sharing, give writers time to look over and reflect on their heart maps. They can either write in their writers' notebooks in response to questions such as the following or discuss them with a partner:

- What do I notice about my heart map?
- What did I discover about myself?
- What surprised me as I mapped my heart?
- What was my process of heart mapping?
- What were some of the feelings that emerged as I mapped my heart?

In Mary Glover's class at the Awakening Seed School, after creating and writing poems from a variety of heart maps, her students reflected and wrote about their process of heart mapping. William chose the Be the Change That You Wish to See in the World heart map and the Gratitude heart map (see Figure 4.2).

After drawing and writing on his My Writer's Heart map, Jonah selected the topic *fiction* from his

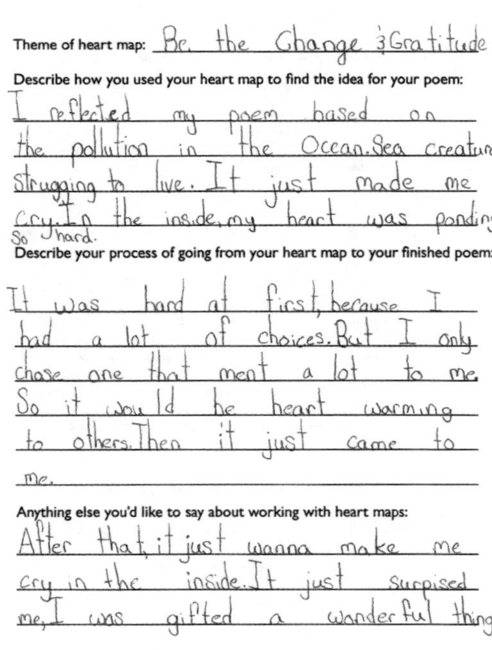

Theme of heart map: Be the Change & Gratitude

Describe how you used your heart map to find the idea for your poem:

I reflected my poem based on the pollution in the Ocean. Sea creatures struggling to live. It just made me cry. In the inside, my heart was ponding so hard.

Describe your process of going from your heart map to your finished poem:

It was hard at first, because I had a lot of choices. But I only chose one that ment a lot to me. So it would be heart warming to others. Then it just came to me.

Anything else you'd like to say about working with heart maps:

After that, it just wanna make me cry in the inside. It just surpised me, I was gifted a wonderful thing.

Figure 4.2 William wrote about how heart mapping brought up sad feelings and yet, despite these deep feelings, mapping his heart also gave him a sense of gratefulness and wonder: *I was gifted a wonderful thing*.

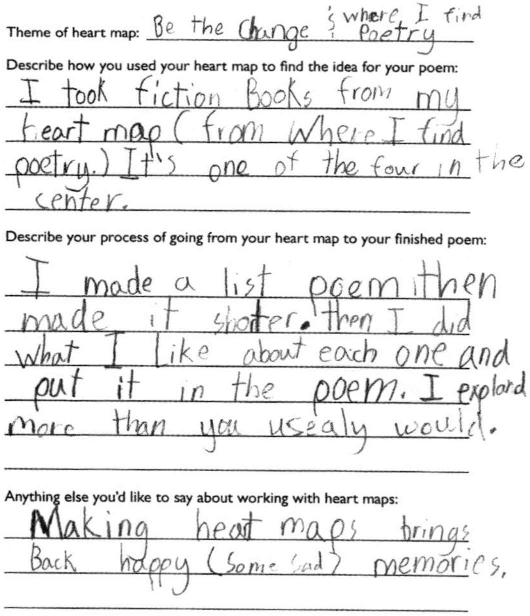

Theme of heart map: Be the Change & where I find Poetry

Describe how you used your heart map to find the idea for your poem:

I took fiction Books from my heart map (from where I find poetry.) It's one of the four in the center.

Describe your process of going from your heart map to your finished poem:

I made a list poem then made it shoter. then I did what I like about each one and put it in the poem. I explord more than you usealy would.

Anything else you'd like to say about working with heart maps:

Making heat maps brings Back happy (Some sad) memories.

Figure 4.3 Jonah then wrote about his process of writing from heart maps

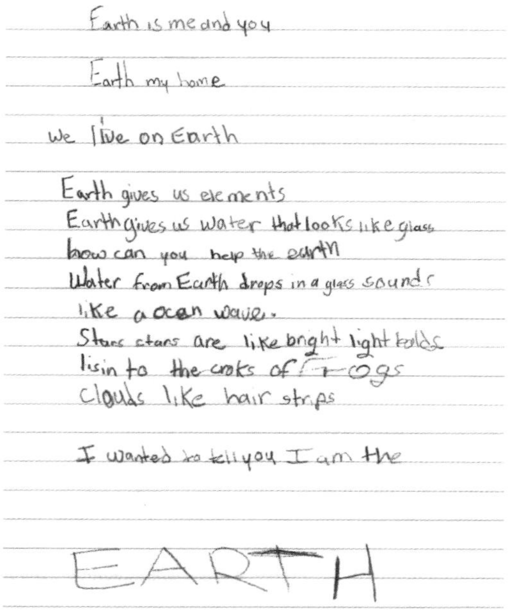

Earth is me and you

Earth my home

we live on Earth

Earth gives us elements
Earth gives us water that looks like glass
how can you help the earth
Water from Earth drops in a glass sounds
like a ocean wave.
Stars stars are like bright light bolds
lisin to the croks of Frogs
clouds like hair strips

I wanted to tell you I am the

EARTH

Figure 4.4 Ede's draft of her poem "How I Give You Life"

heart map to write a poem about. Here is Jonah's poem "Fiction Books." (His heart map was shown in Chapter 3, Figure 3.9.)

Fiction Books

Magical creatures
creeping around the corner . . .
sfuo, sfa,
burn!

Battle cry!

Knights running
into battle.

Carriages clapping
on the rocky roads.

Mystical rings found
in a treasure chest
guarded by a moving tree
with powers.

All in an
author's mind.

Ede focused her Gratitude heart map on the earth, which she placed in the center of her map. After rereading her heart map, she began drafting a poem about the earth (see Figure 4.4).

She then revised her poem, as follows:

How I Give You Life

I give you elements and I give you life.
You were born on me.
I give you water that looks like glass,
airy clouds like hair strips that you see
and not see almost every day.

My son, the Sun, is a fiery star,
like a bright light bulb that gives you
the ability to live.

Listen to the croaks of my living frogs,
in the swamps going hippety-hop,
singing their earth songs and
I wanted to tell you mine:

I am the EARTH.

How can you help me?

Ede then wrote a reflection (see Figure 4.5) about her entire heart-mapping process, saying, *I opened my heart to do this heart map*. She ended with such a pearl of wisdom: *Well . . . heart maps . . . are amazing they tell so much about you.*

Writers can also summarize and generalize feelings and ideas that emerged as they mapped their hearts. Some writers compare and use a metaphor to describe the feelings from heart maps, as in the following poem by a sixth grader.

My Heart

By Denise

My heart is like a highway
Split into four lanes

The cars that drive upon them
Chauffeur my feelings to my brain

There the happy thoughts get shared
And the sad and bad get stored

The memorable and scary thoughts
Are stacked neatly in mind's drawer

When I need a brand new smile
I drive a car up a lane

A funny lane, a happy lane
To store up in my brain

My heart is like a highway
Split up into four lanes

The cars that drive upon them
Chauffeur my feelings to my brain.

Theme of heart map: Gratitude

Describe how you used your heart map to find the idea for your poem:

I used actual liveing things including frogs and others. I opend my heart to do this heart map. My heart map is about Earth.

Describe your process of going from your heart map to your finished poem:

Earth was the big chunk of my poem. Mary and I worked around the ending so it would make sense to the people that will read it.

Anything else you'd like to say about working with heart maps:

Well.... heart maps.... are amazing they tell so much about you.

Figure 4.5 Ede's reflection on her heart mapping process and how she wrote her poem "How I Give You Life"

Three Hearts

Guest Essays

How I gain access to that interior life is what drives me.

—Toni Morrison, "The Site of Memory"

If this book is a heart, then the wise sparks that make the heart beat are the voices and words of my three colleagues and friends who write so eloquently about their heart-mapping experiences with their students. Pam Allyn, Nancie Atwell, and Penny Kittle are some of the truest, most trusted voices writing about children today, and their words have been a lantern for me for many years.

Here, in her essay "LitWorld Heart Stories," Pam Allyn writes about the impact of heart mapping on her LitWorld organization and the children in LitClubs all over the world; in "What Matters," Nancie Atwell describes how heart mapping opened the heart of one of her students, an adolescent boy who was able to explore his heart to write a poem; and in "Tune in to Your Heart Map Playlist," Penny Kittle describes mapping the hidden playlists of the heart with her adolescent students.

Let their writing be an inspiration in teaching our students to write authentically about what matters.

My friend and colleague Pam Allyn, executive director of LitWorld, has been exploring heart mapping in her literacy clubs for many years as a way to inspire writing and build literacy. In early 2016, she sent out a Spring Heart Mapping Initiative invitation for children in LitClubs, working with partner organizations, in nine countries around the world and in the United States. Ana Seastone Stern, the international program director of LitWorld, directed the initiative and sent me an extraordinary collection of heart maps.

The children who created heart maps are from these countries, cities, and towns and work with LitWorld and the following partner organizations:

Ceinode in Accra, Ghana

Center for Development in Ahmedabad, Gujarat, India

Children of Haiti Project and Fondation TOYA in Port-au-Prince, Haiti

Golden Girls Foundation in Kisumu, Kenya

Kenya Education Fund in Kibera, Nairobi, Kenya

Harlem, New York

Otra Cosa Network in Huanchaco Village, Peru

Project PEARLS in Bulacan and Helping Land in Tondo, Philippines

Ready for Reading in Rwinkwavu, Rwanda

Seeds of Hope in Faisalabad, Pakistan

Art of a Child in Kampala, Uganda

In the following essay, Pam Allyn writes about the profound impact heart mapping has had on the children in LitClubs around the world.

LitWorld Heart Stories, by Pam Allyn

Little Angel walks to school on a treacherous path. She sings to herself the stories of her heart to keep herself comforted, for the path is dark and there are many dangers along the way.

Sarit attends school for a few hours in the morning and then works long, grueling hours carrying water to and from her village until it is dark.

Ephraim sets stone upon stone, building a wall in his village, while he dreams of a future where he could be an airplane pilot, soaring many miles above his village, to see the world and learn about it.

Dahlia spent her childhood tending to her sick mother. Now she dreams of a day when she could be the doctor who tends to other women.

None of these children is guaranteed a long-term education or the benefits that literacy could bring to his or her life. Their work is long and hard; their days are complex and difficult. They imagine a life where they could live their dreams, for their hearts beat strongly, full of hope and promise, full of the richness every child possesses deep within. These stories, unfulfilled, are a deep, unutterable loss to both that individual child and each one of us as citizens of this world. What could Angel become if her path opens up before her? What could Sarit do to change the world without any constraints? What gifts would Ephraim contribute to our future? How could Dahlia impact others? Those mysteries and undiscovered gifts are beating in the hearts of every one of our LitWorld chil-

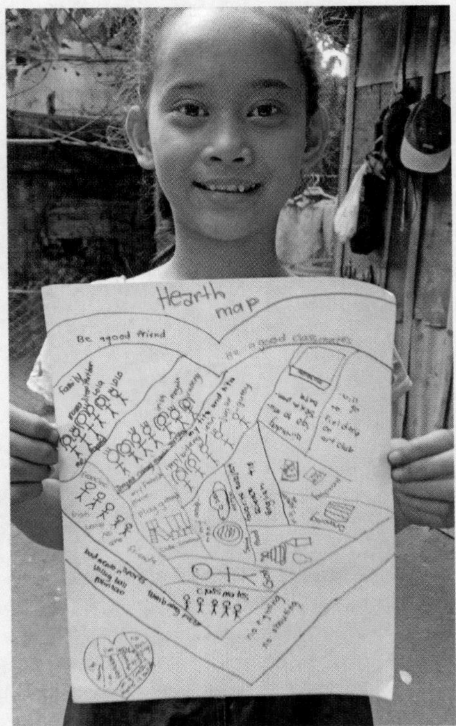

Figure 5.1 A proud heart map creator in Helping Land, Tondo, Manila, Philippines shares people, places, and important things that fill up her heart.

dren nationwide and worldwide, and literacy unlocks them, allows them to burst through, and gives each child the strength to write a new story of possibility.

I founded LitWorld to respond to the urgent challenge of the millions of children who cannot read or write, to create and implement new ways for the world's most marginalized children to have access to the transformational power of reading, writing, and storytelling. Because two-thirds of the world's illiterate people are girls and women, LitWorld dedicates two-thirds of its resources to the work of creating safe spaces and fostering inspirational leadership for girls as writers, readers, and story makers.

In cities in the United States and countries across the globe, young girls and boys gather together each week as members of LitClubs, joyful learning circles that inspire self-confidence and hope. Every LitClub session begins and ends with a song, and members read, write, and—most importantly—*share*. LitClub members know that their voices are not only unique and important but absolutely vital in a world where children's voices, and especially the voices of girls, are too often completely silenced.

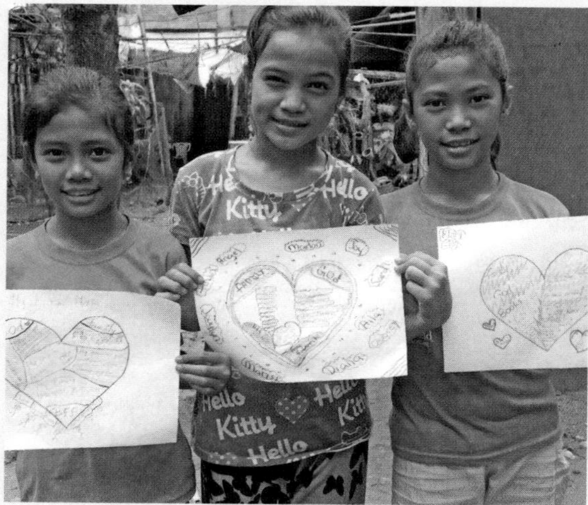

Figure 5.2 Girls of a LitWorld literacy club in Helping Land, Tondo, Manila, Philippines share their heart maps with one another to discover what they have in common and what is unique to their hearts.

Literacy is humankind's greatest innovation. All technology we build and create (whether a click pen or a tablet) is founded on the fundamental human desire to communicate with one another, to hear the stories of the world, and to share the stories of one's own life. The great researcher Paolo Freire said: "For apart from inquiry, apart from the praxis, individuals cannot be truly human. Knowledge emerges only through invention and re-invention, through the restless, impatient, continuing, hopeful inquiry human beings pursue in the world, with the world, and with each other" (2014, 72). Inquiry that comes from exploring new ideas and delving into the corners of one's own heart—this is literacy. And literacy is a human right. LitWorld provides the advocacy and work to make this possible for all children, no matter their zip code or place of birth. Transformational literacy is a human right that belongs to all children.

Georgia Heard's heart maps have created a profound and quietly beautiful way for LitWorld to build a safe and beloved community for literacy from the very first moment our children come together. The lives of our "LitKids" are hard beyond belief. LitWorld works side by side with communities ravaged by storms of poverty, inequity, human conflict, and natural disaster. Be it in the slow, grinding catastrophe of poverty or the sudden, shocking devastation of an earthquake, heart maps help our children, in the midst of these unthinkable odds, express their truest selves and build safe spaces around them for inquiry, learning, and healing. Valuing one's own stories with the tool of literacy is the antidote to oppression, for it gives the child her own active tools to seek knowledge, to be in a state of inquiry about the life she leads, and to begin shaping and crafting goals for her own hopeful future. There are those who would try to convince us that children—girls, especially—should not be in school, should not be learning, and this is often said in the name of religion or custom. We cannot accept this. The girls and boys who write their hopes and dreams and understandings into their heart maps from Detroit to Pakistan to Mississippi to Kenya all hunger for the power to tell their stories and to hear the stories of others. Heart maps, and a child's writing within them, provide windows onto the world and mirrors into the life she wants to see, know, and become.

In Pakistan, girls must cover the windows to hide the fact that they are meeting to learn to read and write. After the earthquake in Nepal, children used heart maps to work through the trauma of watching their homes crumble before their eyes. In the Philippines, girls work long hours pulling nails out of boards to sell precious amounts of metal, their young hands worn and aged long before their time. In Kenya, children live in communities where there is no electricity and the darkness is thick with danger. When these young people turn to the work of their heart maps, their smiles reappear, their

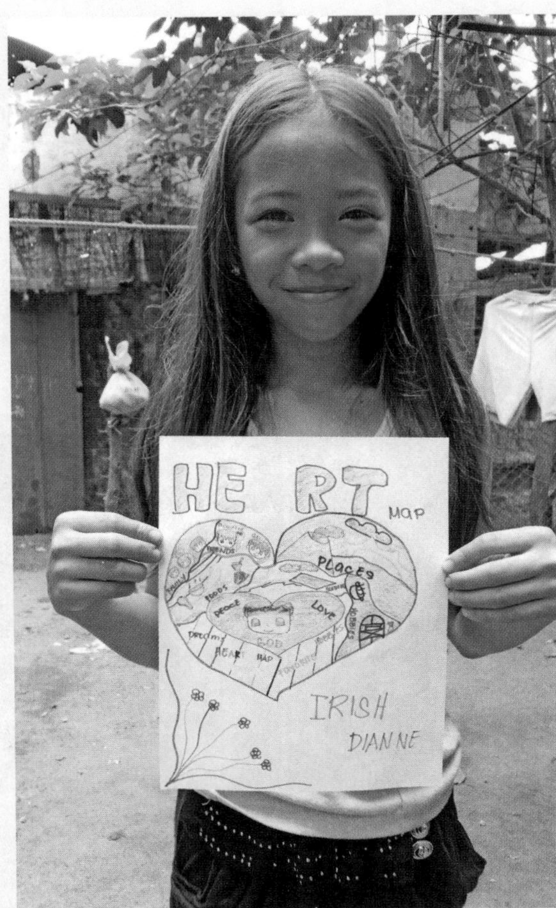

Figure 5.3 By sharing her heart map, Dianne of Helping Land, Tondo, Manila, Philippines offers insight into her world, her hopes, her dreams, her story.

Figure 5.4 The heart map allows children to think visually and literally about what matters to them as shown by this heart map maker in Helping Land, Tondo, Manila, Philippines.

natural hunger for the joys of childhood return, and their real, hopeful selves shine through for all to see.

What may appear as a simple activity is really courage in action. Heart maps portray deeply felt memories, loves, and sorrows—artifacts too often suppressed in children by the forces around them. When a child writes, she gives power to her thoughts and her thoughts can become actions in the world. Words and images inside the map are a representation of all that is resilient and individual and transformational about the human spirit. What is in you is what makes you strong, and in the sharing, you strengthen your community and the world.

The future of our world lies in the dreams of our children. These heart stories empower our children—Angel, Ephraim, Sarit, Dahlia, and so many others—giving them strength on their journeys and the resiliency to write a new story of hope and opportunity in the days to come.

Figure 5.5 A celebratory moment during a LitWorld girls literacy club meeting in Katmandu, Nepal after a joyful heart mapping session.

Figure 5.6 The heart map offers a glimpse into the inner life of a young boy in Port-au-Prince, Haiti.

Figure 5.7 School, dance, playing with friends, the beach. A playful heart map in Haitian Creole created by a child in Port-au-Prince, Haiti.

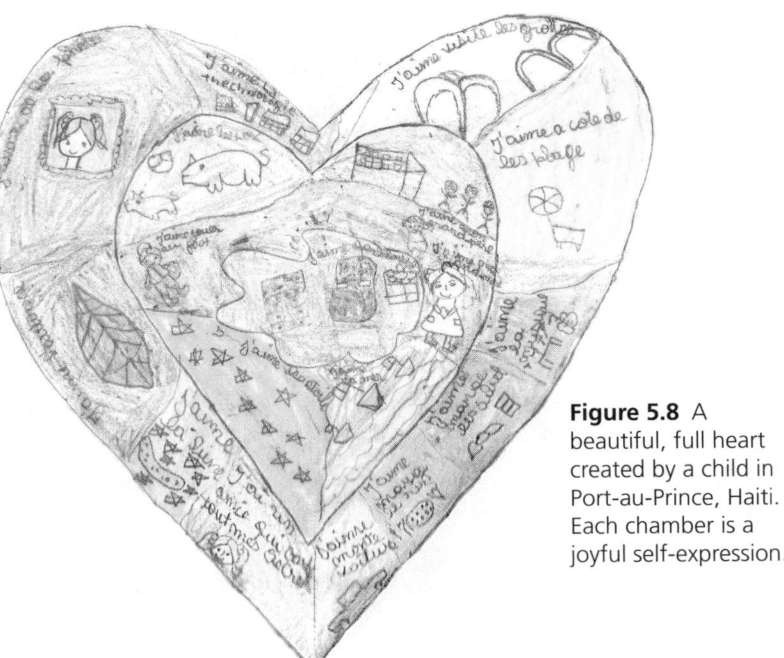

Figure 5.8 A beautiful, full heart created by a child in Port-au-Prince, Haiti. Each chamber is a joyful self-expression.

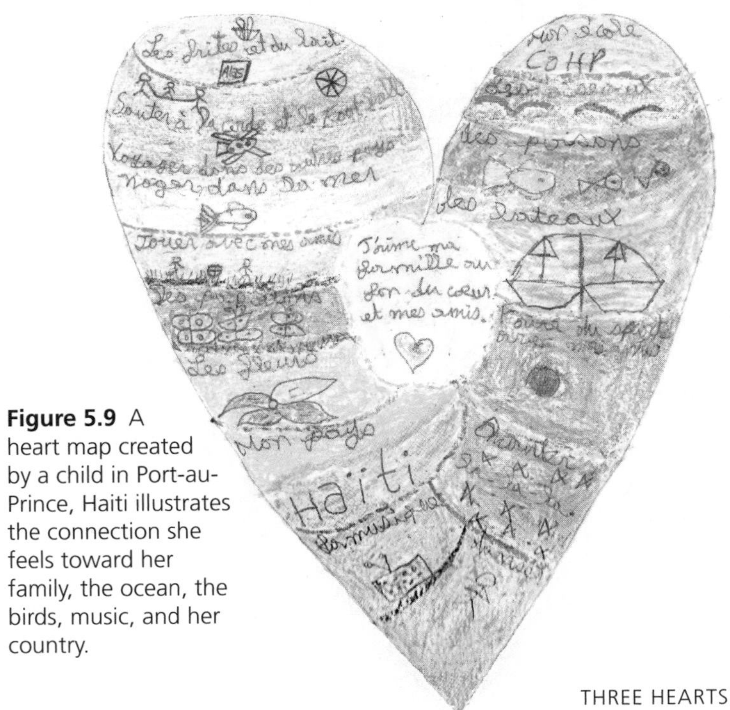

Figure 5.9 A heart map created by a child in Port-au-Prince, Haiti illustrates the connection she feels toward her family, the ocean, the birds, music, and her country.

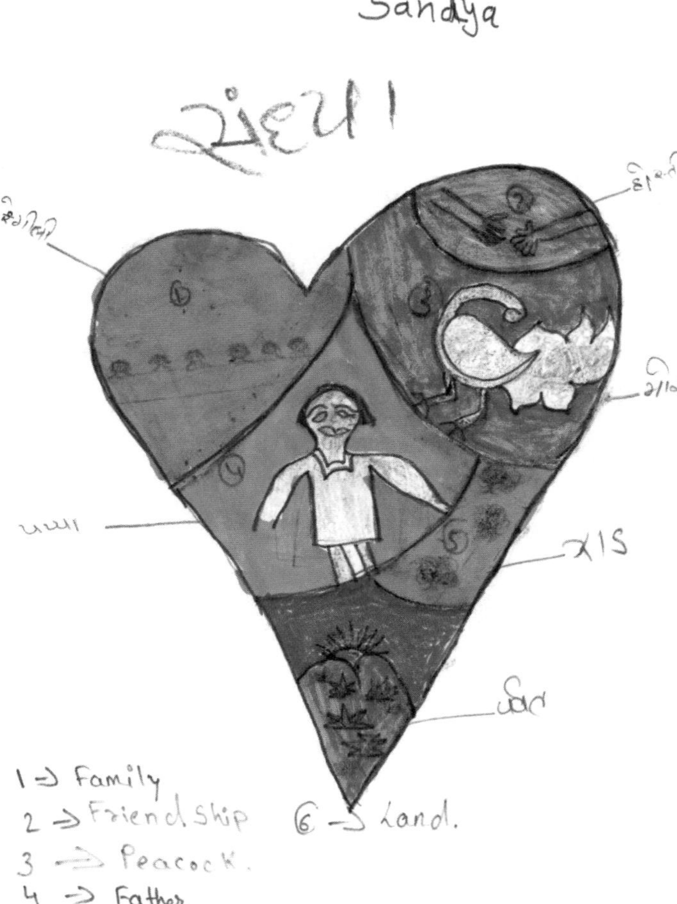

Figure 5.10 A vibrant heart map with a translation key by Sandya of Ahmedabad, Gujarat, India.

Figure 5.11 Sophia in Accra, Ghana uses the heart map activity to stand up for what she believes in, to raise her voice and advocate for issues that matter to her.

Figure 5.12 A heart map from an adolescent in Accra, Ghana demonstrates how heart mapping supports grappling with big questions and times of transition.

Figure 5.13 This heart map written in the Gujarati language and created by Patham in Ahmedabad, Gujarat, India is bursting with passion and curiosity.

Figure 5.14 An emotional heart map from a child in Kenya.

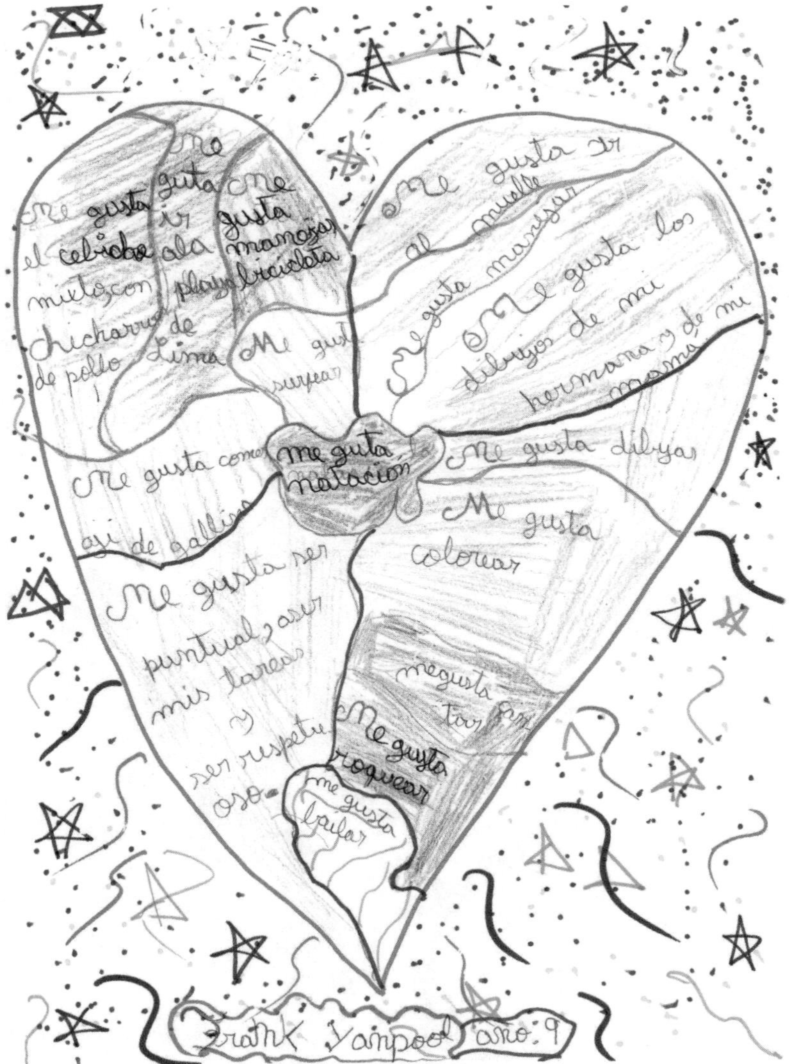

Figure 5.15 The celebratory designs and colors that adorn the heart of nine-year-old Frank of Helping Land, Tondo, Manila Philippines tell us how he feels when he thinks, draws, and writes about the things he loves.

Figure 5.16 A heart map created by Meerib of Faislabad, Pakistan in Urdu is a window to the big questions and wonderings in her life.

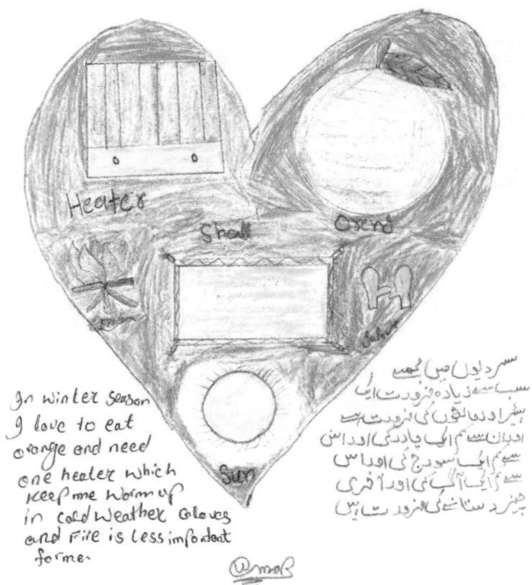

Figure 5.17 The winter heart of a child written in Urdu and English in Faislabad, Pakistan.

Figure 5.18 A child in Rwinkwavu, Rwanda plays with illustration, words written in Kinyarwanda, and use of space in the heart map.

Figure 5.19 The soaring heart of a child in Huanchaco Village, Peru.

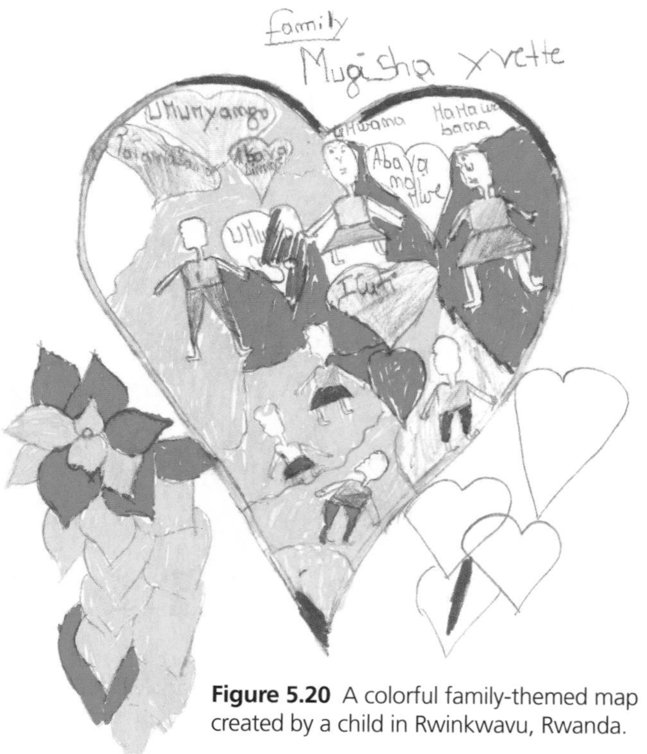

Figure 5.20 A colorful family-themed map created by a child in Rwinkwavu, Rwanda.

Figure 5.21 The heart map of Gloria, a member of a LitWorld literacy club in Kampala, Uganda.

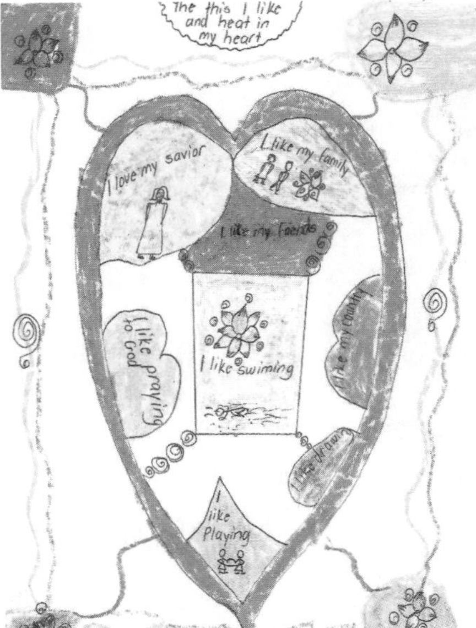

Figure 5.22 A bold and artistic heart map created by a young adult in Kampala, Uganda.

Figure 5.23 Nested hearts make a statement on the heart map written in Kinyarwanda, created by a child in Rwinkwavu, Rwanda.

Figure 5.24 A colorful and intricately labeled heart map by Parmar of Ahmedabad, Gujarat, India written in Gujarati illustrates what she holds dear.

What Matters, by Nancie Atwell

Like most of the poems Carl wrote in eighth grade, "The Bowl" was prompted by a posting on his heart map. Between *Hans's paws* and *potato picking techniques*, using just enough words to capture the memory, he'd written *breaking the red bowl*. When he fleshed out the phrase, it became a poem about family, heritage, love, and regret.

The Bowl

In a second
it leaves my clumsy fingers
and crashes to the floor.
You turn at the sound
to find shards of the little red bowl
scattered across the tile.
I look up from the remains
and watch sadness seep
into your face.
And then I realize:
to me it was the whipped cream bowl,
to you it was a bowl of memories,
a tie to your childhood, your children,
your own mother.
I look down at the pieces
of a life
lying in front of me.
Then I turn
to get
the broom.

—*Carl Johanson*

The conclusion is a simple, strong image of a twelve-year-old boy who recognizes that sometimes there aren't words. No apology will suffice; the little bowl was that big to his mother. All he can do is sweep up the mess he made. But he did give "The Bowl" to her, and she loved it. Carl's mom told me she hadn't realized he'd understood what it had meant to her. She was touched by his empathy and grateful to both of us.

I, in turn, was grateful to Georgia. Carl would never have written the poem if he hadn't charted the experiences, people, places, and things that resonated for him, that helped make Carl *Carl*. The process of mining his heart pulled buried treasure to the surface and made it accessible to him to write about.

Heart maps work for all kids, but their impact on boys is remarkable. The feelings of my male students are just as strong as those of their female classmates, but guys don't always have the language or an opportunity to express them. I remember being approached one day after school by another mother of boys, two taciturn, woodsman types. "I can't get over their poetry," she said. "I didn't know they had all this inside them—all these things they think about and notice and feel."

To encourage kids to go deep and be deep as poets and heart mappers, I introduce the process by mining the contents of my own heart (see Figure 5.25). I make sure the entries are particular and evocative. If I

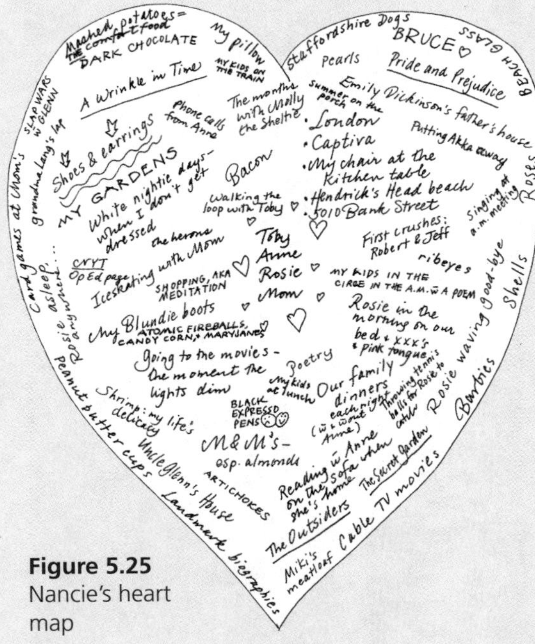

Figure 5.25
Nancie's heart map

Questions to Elicit Topics for Kindergartners' Heart Maps

Favorite toys?
Favorite stuffie?
Your dog?
Your cat?
Another pet?
Favorite color?
Your bedroom?
Your mom?
Your dad?
Your grandma?
Your grandpa?
Your aunt?
Your uncle?
Your cousin(s)?
Your little or big brother or sister?
Your imaginary friend?
Your first lost or loose tooth?
The first holiday you remember?
Favorite game?
Favorite song?
Favorite shoes? Pajamas? Shirt?
A favorite trip?
A favorite book?
Favorite holiday?
Favorite Halloween costume?
Favorite wild animal?
Favorite dinner?
Favorite candy?
Favorite drink?
Favorite store?
Your best friends?
Your first day of school?
Favorite season?
Favorite day of the week?
Favorite music?
Favorite thing to do in the summer?
Favorite thing(s) to do in the snow?
Favorite places at your house inside?
Favorite places at your house outside?
Favorite things to do after school?
A special thing your family always does on someone's birthday? At Christmas?

Figure 5.26 Kindergarten question list

show students a heart filled with general categories—*favorite foods* instead of *mashed potatoes as comfort food*, *rib eyes*, and *Atomic FireBalls*, or *reading* instead of *The Secret Garden*, *A Wrinkle in Time*, *The Outsiders*, and *Pride and Prejudice*—they record categories, too, and then they either don't find ideas that inspire them or produce clichéd bromides about topics like friends, candy, and pets. I'm pretty sure that Carl's entry *Hans's paws* was triggered by my note about Rosie's pink tongue. A good heart map helps a poet identify and consider what matters to him or her alone.

I also take care not to go too far in the other direction in my demonstration. Plumbing the meaning of an entry comes later, during the act of writing about it. If a teacher requires students to delve into the significance of every idea they post, the generative power of heart mapping is checked. Not every topic will represent an itch worth scratching as a poem, but the act of recording an un-scratch-worthy idea often leads to recording one that's worthwhile. Heart mapping should feel exciting and intriguing to kids—an opportunity to play wholeheartedly in answer to the overarching question, "What has stayed in my heart?"

I created a list of subordinate questions to help kids be specific in their answers. They tape it to the bottom corner of the page on which they draw an outline of their heart and consult it to prompt a variety of discoveries.

Questions to Help Mine Your Heart

What has *stayed there*? What moments, family members, pets, obsessions, adventures, animals, objects, places, books, fears, scars, friends, teachers, things to eat and drink, journeys, secrets, dreams, delights, crushes, comforts, toys, tragedies, traditions? What's at the center? The edges? What has stayed in your heart?

At my K–8 school, the Center for Teaching and Learning, student poets answer the question every year; seventh and eighth graders interview the kindergartners to help them fill in their first heart maps (see Figure 5.26). As children grow up, they make new memories, and their vision of what matters changes and grows, too. Carl's entry *breaking the red bowl* emerged only on the heart map he created as an eighth grader.

Last year, a decade after Carl wrote "The Bowl," I heard from his mother once again. The occasion was my retirement as a classroom teacher. She sent me a note that concluded, "Through poems like the one about the broken red bowl, you strengthen our family in love. Although the bowl is long gone, we have the poem."

The lost heirloom was exchanged for another, a poem that perpetuated its memory and created a new one for Carl's family. The power of all art, poetry in general, and heart mapping in particular, is how it captures, illuminates, and sustains what matters.

Tune in to Your Heart Map Playlist, by Penny Kittle

Music unlocks memories.

Pachelbel's Canon in D Major puts me at the back of a church on a snowy December Saturday, trembling as I hold my father's hand. He pats my arm and says, "Easy now," as we start toward the altar.

When a song I once labored to learn on my guitar comes on the radio it transports me to Oregon State's campus, and I see a swirl of fall color as I walk from class with my black guitar case bumping my leg in a bouncing rhythm. I'm twenty again and the year suddenly returns to me in images, feelings, and songs.

Our hearts hold hidden playlists.

When I create heart map playlists with students, they access moments that might become poems or memoirs or even the anchors to essays they didn't realize were inside of them, waiting to be written.

A heart's playlist is more than a list of titles. We sort them as we freely find and list bits of lyrics. At the center are the songs most precious to us and on the outside edge are the ones we once loved but have grown tired of. Some students have listed tunes they wished they could forget outside of their hearts—like those advertising jingles that stubbornly repeat and annoy. Amelya split the heart in half and listed songs and concerts she has shared with her dad on one side and the songs her mom sings while cooking on the other.

Once we've listed for several minutes I have students select one song to quickly write about—to make it the soundtrack to a story they want to relive line upon line. And yes, they can put headphones on and write with the song playing to deepen their remembering, as I often do myself. Some students adopt headphones as a regular part of their writing routine in class, allowing music to help them block out distractions and draft more easily. I know this move as a writer: I've created a playlist for every book I've written. The familiarity of notes relaxes me and I sink into words.

The music heart map led Joe back to fishing with his father. He filled his notebook with pages of memories, finding that the words themselves led him to the details of a time long past. This was a turning point for his engagement in my class, in the hard work of writing, and in the satisfaction of finding something he wanted to say well as he labored over revision and rethinking. And music led Hannah to a forgotten innocence—her twelve-year-old self belted in the backseat next to her best friend, singing along to music from the Broadway show *Wicked*. The friendship had ended, but the bitterness of that was suddenly replaced by memories of that friendship's value in her life.

My students and I discover the gift of a heart map playlist: to soothe, to comfort, to remind us of the beauty in our past and in our daily living.

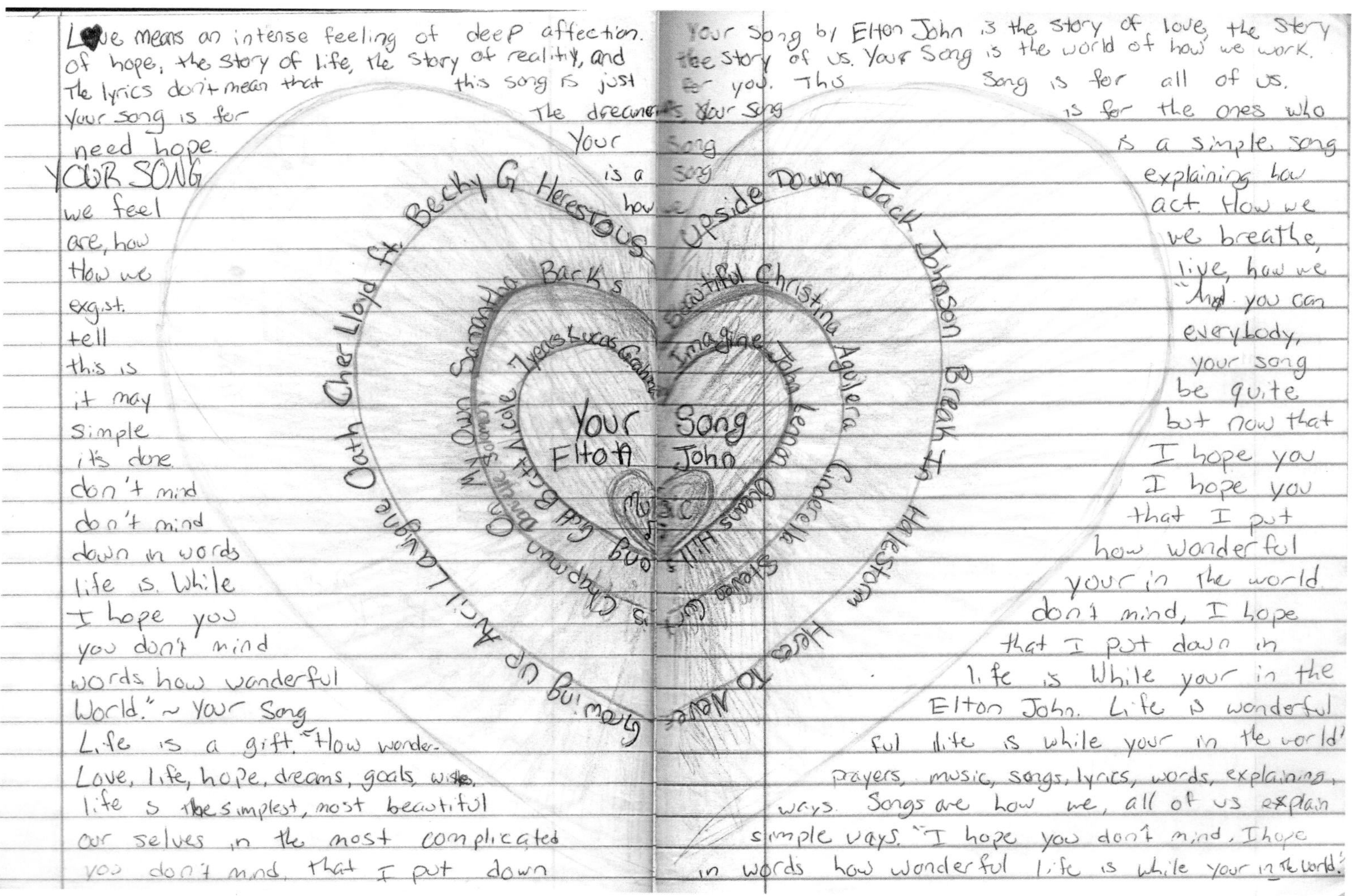

Figure 5.27 Danielle's playlist heart map

Epilogue: Keeping Our Hearts Open

Thou shalt fall in love at least three times a day.

—MATTHEW FOX

In the early morning when I go for a walk with my husband and dog, I wake myself up and creak my heart open by deliberately falling in love with the world in all its detail: brown snails slinking slowly across the sidewalk; the ocean's muted roar a mile away; a sticky green frog hopping up the front door. Arriving back home, I open the door and my heart leaps as I see my seventeen-year-old son just waking up, at 6 feet 4 inches, towering above me, and I wonder how he grew up so fast.

I try to remember the advice from Matthew Fox to fall in love three times a day. When we pay attention, when we live our lives as wide-awake humans, we open our hearts. When we move beyond to-do lists and routine, we can transform the ordinary into the enchanted. We have to be brave and vulnerable enough to dig deep.

My hope is that as you explore heart mapping with your writers, you will fall in love with the stories and poems, truths and courage that will unfold—both theirs and your own.

Heart Work

In September,
words lay still
and silent inside your hearts.
If you listened carefully,
you might have heard
the quivering of wings.
Then from the corner
of your eye, you could have spied
a flutter or two—
words slowly
unfolding,
delicate, silken wings.
Soon, stories and poems
appeared everywhere.
Rainbow wings beating, flapping,
hovering over desks, hanging
from the ceiling, tips of noses, tops of heads.
It was difficult to get any work done!
Now, your words
fly free. You fold memories
in your hearts.
Small butterflies raised,
watched, and let loose
into the world.

—*Georgia Heard*

Works Cited

Bartholomae, David. 1983. "Writing Assignments: Where Writing Begins." In *FORUM: Essays on Theory and Practice in the Teaching of Writing*, edited by Patricia Stock, 300–12. Portsmouth, NH: Boynton/Cook.

Calkins, Lucy. 2013. *Units of Study in Opinion, Information, and Narrative Writing, Grades K–5*. Portsmouth, NH: Heinemann.

———. 2014. *Units of Study in Argument, Information, and Narrative Writing, Grades 6–8*. Portsmouth, NH: Heinemann.

Fanelli, Sara. 2001. *My Map Book*. New York: HarperFestival.

Fletcher, Ralph. 2007. *How to Write Your Life Story*. New York: Collins.

Fox, John. 1997. "When Someone Deeply Listens to You." In *Poetic Medicine: The Healing Art of Poem-Making*. New York: Jeremy T. Tarcher Putnam.

Freiro, Paulo. 2014. *Pedagogy of the Oppressed: 30th Anniversary Edition*. New York: Bloomsbury Academics.

Grudin, Robert. 1990. *The Grace of Great Things: Creativity and Innovation*. Boston: Ticknor and Fields.

Heard, Georgia. 1995. *Writing Toward Home: Tales and Lessons to Find Your Way*. Portsmouth, NH: Heinemann.

———. 1999. *Awakening the Heart: Exploring Poetry in Elementary and Middle School*. Portsmouth, NH: Heinemann.

———. 2012. "The Winner." In *The Poetry Friday Anthology: Poems for the School Year with Connections to the Common Core, K–5 Edition*, edited by Sylvia Vardell and Janet Wong, 109. Princeton, NJ: Pomelo Books.

———. 2013. *Finding the Heart of Nonfiction: Teaching 7 Essential Craft Tools with Mentor Texts*. Portsmouth, NH: Heinemann.

Heard, Georgia, and Lester Laminack. 2007. *Climb Inside a Poem: Reading and Writing Poetry Across the Year*. Portsmouth: FirstHand/Heinemann.

Hurwitz, Johanna. 1997. *Helen Keller: Courage in the Dark*. New York: Random House Books for Young Readers.

Johnston, Bret Anthony. 2011. "Don't Write What You Know: Why Fiction's Narrative and Emotional Integrity Will Always Transcend the Literal Truth." *The Atlantic* (Fiction 2011 issue). www.theatlantic.com/magazine/archive/2011/08/dont-write-what-you-know/308576/

Johnston, Tony. 1990. *The Quilt Story*. New York: Scholastic.

Keene, Ellin. 2012. *Talk About Understanding: Rethinking Classroom Talk to Enhance Comprehension*. Portsmouth, NH: Heinemann.

Korb, Alex. 2012. "The Grateful Brain: The Neuroscience of Giving Thanks." *Psychology Today* November 20. www.psychologytoday.com/blog/prefrontal-nudity/201211/the-grateful-brain.

Kourndian, Haig. 2012. "Learning Through Visuals: Visual Imagery in the Classroom." *Get Psyched!* (blog), July 20. www.psychologytoday.com/blog/get-psyched/201207/learning-through-visuals

Martin, Lee. 2011. "Discovering What Lies Beneath: An Interview with Lee Martin." By Dawn Haines. *Brevity* (January). http://brevitymag.com/craft-essays/discovering-what-lies-beneath-an-interview-with-lee-martin/

———. 2012. "From the Fiction Workshop: Week 4." *Lee Martin* (blog), January 15. http://leemartinauthor.com/2012/01/from-the-fiction-workshop-week-4/

———. 2015. "Close to Home: Writing the Small and the Intimate." *Lee Martin* (blog), October 12. http://leemartinauthor.com/2015/10/close-to-home-writing-the-small-and-the-intimate/

McCullough, David. 1999. "David McCullough, the Art of Biography No. 2." Interviewed by Elizabeth Gaffney and Benjamin Ryder Howe. *The Paris Review* (Fall). www.theparisreview.org/interviews/894/the-art-of-biography-no-2-david-mccullough

———. 2003. "David McCullough Interview: The Title Always Comes Last." By Bruce Cole. National Endowment for the Humanities. www.neh.gov/about/awards/jefferson-lecture/david-mccullough-interview

Meltzer, Milton. 1976. "Where Do All the Prizes Go? The Case for Nonfiction." *The Horn Book Magazine* (February).

Olien, Rebecca. 2012. *Map Keys*. New York: Scholastic.

Polacco, Patricia. 2001. *The Keeping Quilt*. New York: Simon and Schuster/Paula Wiseman Books.

Quercia, Daniele. 2014. "Happy Maps." *TED Talks* (podcast), November. www.ted.com/talks/daniele_quercia_happy_maps?language=en

Rilke, Rainer Maria. 1989. *The Selected Poetry of Rainer Maria Rilke*. Translated by Stephen Mitchell. New York: Vintage.

Soto, Gary. 1996. *Too Many Tamales*. New York: Puffin Books.

Stafford, William. 1990. Commentary on "One Time." In *The Place My Words Are Looking For: What Poets Say About and Through Their Work*, selected by Paul Janeczko, 59. New York: Simon and Schuster Books for Young Readers.

Superville, Darlene. 2015. "Obama: World Would Be 'Pretty Barren' Without Poetry." *Cnsnews.com*, April 17. www.cnsnews.com/news/article/obama-world-would-be-pretty-barren-without-poetry

Walker, Alice. 1983. "Beauty: When the Other Dancer Is the Self." In *In Search of Our Mothers' Gardens: Womanist Prose*. San Diego: Harcourt Brace Jovanovich.

Woolf, Virginia. 1976. *Flush: A Biography*. New York: Mariner Books.